JOHN KEATS' FANCY

JOHN KEATS' FANCY

THE EFFECT ON KEATS OF THE PSYCHOLOGY OF HIS DAY

BY JAMES RALSTON CALDWELL

1965
OCTAGON BOOKS, INC.
New York

Reprinted 1965
by special arrangement with Cornell University Press

OCTAGON BOOKS, INC.
175 FIFTH AVENUE
NEW YORK, N. Y. 10010

LIBRARY OF CONGRESS CATALOG CARD NUMBER: 65-25886

Printed in U.S.A. by
NOBLE OFFSET PRINTERS, INC.
NEW YORK 3, N. Y.

This book is for

JOSEPH RALSTON CALDWELL *and*

JOSEPHINE ELIZABETH CALDWELL

19547

FORENOTE

I HOPE THIS BOOK will interest other thoughtful readers of Keats as well as professional scholars. Partly for this reason I have kept scholarly apparatus at a minimum, indicating my sources and authorities for the most part in the text as I go along, and by titles rather than pages, editions, etc.; but it has seemed to me also that the usual furnishings were not needed in a book of this kind, wherein most of the documents referred to are familiar and accessible to scholars, and the argument does not turn on textual minutiae. Quotations from Keats' poetry (I share Professor Garrod's antipathy to Keats's) are, with one exception, from *The Poetical Works of John Keats,* ed. M. B. Forman (2d ed., New York: Oxford University Press, 1935), whence also I have taken all passages quoted from Keats' letters. The numbers in parenthesis following these passages refer to pages of this edition.

Much of Chapter Four is a rehandling of material which has already appeared in my article, "Beauty Is Truth," in *Five Studies in Literature* (University of California Publications in English, Vol. VIII, No. 1, 1940), and I thank the University of California Press for allowing me to re-use this material here. I am grateful also to my dear friends and colleagues, Professors

Josephine Miles, Benjamin Lehman, Willard H. Durham, Bertrand Bronson, Donald Mackay, and Myron Brightfield, for reading and valuably criticizing this study. I am most of all indebted to Katherine Field Caldwell, who has listened patiently and counseled well.

J. R. C.

CONTENTS

JOHN KEATS' FANCY

"The vaunted verse a vacant head demaundes."

—EDMUND SPENSER

CHAPTER ONE

THE MIND'S
METHOD

T HE INTELLECTUAL IDENTITY
of a poet, or a huckster, consists in how, more than in what,
he thinks. His knowledge, beliefs, philosophies may be superficial and temporary arrangements. They are possessions usually shared. Animating these forms with unique and subtle
energies are the native impulse and peculiar temper of his mind.
To detect these in a poet and describe their working is certainly a most difficult task. For it requires, ideally, that we
observe a mind in motion, that we witness or reconstruct creative acts, and these, since they are complicated, private, and
unique events which have occurred at some time in the past,
we can neither witness nor truly reproduce. Not even the
artist's self can record all the swift constellations of image and
concept as they flash and resolve on the horizon of his creative
hour, nor abstract from this pregnant chaos the cogent, shaping energies. Much less may critics hope to reconstruct them.
The very coil and stress of mind whereby great art comes to
pass are mysteries, "curtained," as Shelley said, "within the
invisible nature of man."

Yet there are paths leading toward these mysteries, paths

indicated sometimes by the poets themselves. For some poets are self-conscious workers, vividly aware of the movements of their own minds, delighted in the experience of thinking and in the act of making poetry, and willing to speak thereof. From them we are able to gather some knowledge of these shrouded, vital events.

John Keats is such a poet. The work-ways of his mind in making poems and in general employment are unusually open, and remarkable; and they have been strangely neglected. I think for two reasons, mainly. First, it took criticism the best part of a century to decide that Keats had any mind worth mentioning, that he was not a purely sensuous man—whatever that phrase could mean of one who regularly "dined on words." And, second, when long study had at last established the fact that he had "philosophy" as well as "sensations," a great deal of energy was at once directed to discovering what this philosophy was, and how it grew. His poems were ransacked for allegorical comment; his generalizations in verse and prose abstracted, scanned, and compared. For this effort, carried on with great pains and learning, we must be deeply grateful. It has laid forever the ghost of the purely sensuous Keats, incapable of cerebration. It has restored the reality of a consciousness normally aware, and rich in various contents. But it has raised meanwhile a legion of tenuous meanings, convictions, philosophies, bewildering in their multitude and swift succession (supposedly) in his mind's center. Keats seems in these researches to have been as over-urged for thoughts and reasons as the honest urchin in Words-worth's "Anecdote for Fathers," and, like him, made to fib by the exigency of his too rational elders.

"At Kilve there was no weather-cock;
And that's the reason why!"

For example, the most recent and detailed history of his intellect, *The Evolution of Keats's Poetry* by Prof. Claude Lee
Finney, conducts him along a sequence of philosophies made
to flash across his mind like views of streets from a train win-
dow: "Optimistic naturalism," given up in the first days of
April, 1817, for "Neo-Platonism," modified by autumn to
"empirical humanism," in turn developed by the end of December to "negative capability," this rejected by March 13
for "scepticism," which slips in the next twelve days to "pes-
simism," displaced on precisely the twenty-fourth of April by
"Wordsworthian humanitarianism," left behind on Oc-
tober 27 for a return to "negative capability."

This account of a mental career checkered to the point of
disrepute is impressively documented, and in a sense doubtless true. But it is also misleading. It tends to take us away
from the realization of a mind infinitely supple, fluent, and
diverse, toward a concept of one merely restless in a succession
of comfortless attitudes; from a brain teeming, as Keats called
his own, toward one jerking fom one static arrangement to
another with the abrupt and angular movement of a kaleido-
scope. The terms and the account provided in this and similar
histories of the poet's mind indicate intellectual structures too
stable and ponderous to reflect the animate, nimble configura-
tions which the poems and letters reveal. What in fact
emerges, indirectly, from this industry is a new awareness of
the tendency to which Keats himself confessed, of indifference to systems of philosophy, a light inconstancy of belief in
reasoned hypotheses on the nature of life:

I do not think myself more in the right than other people, and that nothing in this world is proveable. . . .
Now my dear fellow I must once for all tell you I have
not one Idea of the truth of any of my speculations—I
shall never be a Reasoner because I care not to be in the
right, when retired from bickering and in a proper philosophical temper (111–112).

"Not one word I ever utter," he once wrote, "can be taken
for granted as an opinion growing out of my identical nature.
. . . I have no nature" (228).

This truant habit of mind has brought on much letting of
ink. It has been called mere infirmity, a kind of schizophrenia
which, as much as love, consumption, or the *Quarterly* "so
savage and tartarly," killed him. It has itself been described as
a theory, a "philosophy of negative capability," and fitted into
the rather wildly eventful succession mentioned above. It has
been perhaps more plausibly described as a peculiar movement
of "advance and recoil, progress and reaction and interaction,
an irregular, pendulum-like movement," whereby his mind
progressed from belief to belief. But a better explanation is
surely possible.

Keats was indeed a thoughtful man, but he looked upon
his thoughts with the vivid and reserved gaze of the artist.
His cordial consciousness, though it entertained in its time
many a guest, gave the key to none that was recalcitrant or
extraneous to poetry. A pleasing labyrinth of thought he explored with the same curious joy with which he walked in
his little sister's garden at Walthamstow, "apricot-nibbling,
peach-scrunching, nectarine-sucking," but his purposes and

conduct there were special. *Negative Capability,* "that is, when a man is capable of being in uncertainties, mysteries, doubts, without any irritable reaching after fact," although perversely called a philosophy and discovered to have a "source," was surely a native virtue of his mind. What really absorbed Keats were not the ordered, logical summaries of experience-in-general to be found in philosophies, systems of values, conclusions. These he was but fitfully concerned either to construct or to maintain. Rather it was his own rich experience in creating, exploring, and communicating poetic events. In the vivid foreground of his mind was ever one problem, the problem of making poetry.

But we must not imagine, therefore, that Keats was naïve or incapable of theoretical and systematic thinking, that his delight in the mind was *pleyn delyt,* merely. Ideas interested him deeply but ever in proportion as they shed light on poetry. He looked to them eagerly, not for self-consistency, nor for comprehensive truth, but for use in his work. Now, there were accessible to Keats some rather new and attractive ideas about the mind, and about poetry, ideas that were emphatically usable. He lived in the exciting childhood of psychology. The air he breathed was stirred by the sound of its phrases, illumined, as men believed, by its discoveries, and some of these were very pertinent to the problems of poetry. To such theories naturally he responded. Yet his response was mainly untheoretical. He grasped and used them; hence they soon ceased to be theories and became instead mere ways of going to work. It is the purpose of this book to show that ideas derived from the psychology of his day were of radical importance in Keats' creative life, to observe how these ideas affected his work-ways, and thus better to understand his poetry.

The psychology was the psychology of the association of ideas. Very definitely, although never without the proof of his own experience, it affected Keats' method of composition; he translated its aesthetic formulae in vivid adventures of the imagination; he assimilated and adapted the course of thinking and imagining it described to his own unique and daring uses, exploring, under its sanction, certain hinterlands of the mind, modes of composition and communication never before quite so boldly attempted; and, in the course of his adventures in ways of the imagination, he discovered what seemed to him at once its true use and an answer to the very riddle of life.

These facts we intend to observe. It is clear that the focus of our undertaking will be somewhat narrow. No pretense is made to a complete account of Keats' mind, and we shall leave mostly unmentioned those many "philosophical" ideas which he undoubtedly, in casual fashion, entertained. Some of these, it must be said, appear to be inimical and contradictory (and in that sense, of course, importantly related) to those ideas it will be our special task here to trace in him. Even these apparent gainsayings we shall be but little concerned to explain or reconcile. The view taken in these pages is that the ideas here explored were central in Keats' mind, even though not always undisturbed there, that the use of the mind here described was one practiced, if not invariably, at least frequently and on great occasions. On this assumption we shall be content merely to try to understand these ideas and uses and mark their consequence in Keats' work rather than attempt to place them in a context of other and apparently less relevant conceptions.

THE BARDIC TRANCE

When Keats wrote to his fellow poet, John Hamilton Reynolds, "axioms in philosophy are not axioms until they are proven upon our pulses," he stated at once a principle of good art, and a profound truth of his own nature. The fine resolve to take nothing as foregranted, to write only of things "felt in the blood, and felt along the heart" was firm in his conscience and early made. It speaks, of course, in the intensity and sincerity of all his best poems, but also, in slightly different wise in his early ones, including those in his first (1817) volume, which are most of them not his best. What was there on the pulses of the twenty-one-year-old boy, fresh from the apothecary's shop and the hospital wards, to make into honest poetry? Love, sorrow, death, and the occult fusion of pain and pleasure in beauty were to strike in their time, but they had not yet invaded his heart. Meanwhile there were nature, books, friends. But most especially there was the experience of making poems, the controlled delirium of composition, the startling upsurge of the mind in labor. This was the new wonder, the moving, personal event which, as it increased in frequency and intensity through the end of 1815, and through the year 1816, more and more absorbed him. Of this he could speak; and in approximately one poem out of every three written between November and April, does speak in more or less detail.

What he says provides an easy lesson in the difference between a theory of composition and a theory taken into the blood stream of a poet and warmed there to life. It is a description of making poetry which, taken surfacewise, is axiomatic, but it is also a description—though not literal—of something that actually occurred when Keats made poetry. The description appears oftenest in the form of a recurrent image of the Ideal Poet caught up in the creative trance. Behind this dominant image, we can see the shape of Keats' own practice, and we can complete the details from direct accounts (his own and others) in prose and verse, which supposedly describe certain actual experiences or habits of composition. We can eke out this information, finally, with evidence less intentional, and perhaps thereby more valuable, of other creative events.

Keats' image of the ideal poet emerges succinctly in a sonnet Amy Lowell discovered in the Morgan collection and first published in 1924. Woodhouse dates it "about 1815/6." The philosophy of composition it reveals in outline appears consistently in the early poems.

THE POET

At morn, at noon, at Eve, and Middle Night
  He passes forth into the charmed air,
   With talisman to call up spirits rare
From plant, cave, rock, and fountain.—To his sight
The hush of natural objects opens quite
   To the core: and every secret essence there
   Reveals the elements of good and fair;
Making him see, where Learning hath no light.

Sometimes above the gross and palpable things
   Of this diurnal sphere, his spirit flies
   On awful wing; and with its destined skies
Holds premature and mystic communings:
   Till such unearthly intercourses shed
   A visible halo round his mortal head.

The badness of this sonnet has been duly remarked and rebuked. The notion of "inspiration" which it indicates is said to be imitative of Hunt and Wordsworth. It is, nevertheless, after we have discounted the awestruck and sentimental tone of it and admitted the triteness of the concept, an outline of Keats' own theory and practice of poetry, a practice which was demonstrably unconventional and vivid. According to this account, the poet is stimulated by an experience in nature. He can by a special gift derive from this physical stimulus much more than mere sensations—even abstract ideas of goodness and beauty—and much more than is permitted to the learned mind, set in the ordinary molds of thinking. Sometimes he is borne far away from the sensory experiences to a sense of ultimate verities.

The sonnet "On Leaving Some Friends at an Early Hour" presents the same image in the form of a wish.

Give me a golden pen, and let me lean
   On heap'd up flowers, in regions clear, and far;
   Bring me a tablet whiter than a star,
Or hand of hymning angel, when 'tis seen
The silver strings of heavenly harp atween:
   And let there glide by many a pearly car,
   Pink robes, and wavy hair, and diamond jar,
And half discovered wings, and glances keen.

The while let music wander round my ears,
  And as it reaches each delicious ending,
    Let me write down a line of glorious tone,
  And full of many wonders of the spheres:
    For what a height my spirit is contending!
    'Tis not content so soon to be alone.

In these moments of creative ecstasy, the mind of the poet is passive to the procession of visions moving across it. Conscious intellection, guidance of the course of images, what we call "thought," have no apparent place in the event. The impact of the physical beauties of nature starts the poet on a spontaneous and inconsequent mental process which gathers emotional momentum as it goes forward, and which carries him to heights of speculation, to insights valid in some profound sense. The experience is described again in the "Epistle to My Brother George," this time with playful overtones:

But there are times, when those that love the bay,
Fly from all sorrowing far, far away;
A sudden glow comes on them. . . .

      .   .   .   .   .   .

. . . when a Poet is in such a trance,
In air he sees white coursers paw, and prance.

      .   .   .   .   .   .

These wonders strange he sees, and many more,
Whose head is pregnant with poetic lore.
Should he upon an evening ramble fare
With forehead to the soothing breezes bare,
Would he naught see but the dark, silent blue
With all its diamonds trembling through and through?
Or the coy moon, when in the waviness

Of whitest clouds she does her beauty dress,
And staidly paces higher up, and higher,
Like a sweet nun in holy-day attire?
Ah, yes! much more would start into his sight—
The revelries, and mysteries of night.

In a poem at which we shall soon look closely the point is
made that specific objects of nature inspire poetry consonant
in tone and quality with these objects:

In the calm grandeur of a sober line,
We see the waving of the mountain pine;
And when a tale is beautifully staid,
We feel the safety of a hawthorn glade.
        —"I stood tip-toe upon a little hill"

And in a passage deleted in the manuscript:

Men's thoughts have sure been winged   They have found
An inspiration in a pleasant sound
Or pleasant sight.

Keats then explains the origin of myth according to the same
principle:

What first inspired a bard of old to sing
Narcissus pining o'er the untainted spring?
In some delicious ramble, he had found
A little space, with boughs all woven round;
And in the midst of all, a clearer pool
Than e'er reflected in its pleasant cool
The blue sky here, and there, serenely peeping.

Particular sights, sounds, smells, in other words, are the breeders of literature, especially of myth.

Most of this seems on the face of it trite enough. The view of poetry as a process of direct divination, as composed in a kind of trance or rapture, fostered by getting out of doors, the emotional excitement, the visions, the soaring to heights of ethereal knowledge and beauty are all perfectly conventional. From Plato's *Ion* down there is scarcely a critic who does not pay at least a service of lip to original genius, the poet's rage, and range and insight. These operations are ascribed to a superrational faculty, sometimes called the imagination, sometimes the fancy. Thomas Fuller, the seventeenth-century author of *The History of the Worthies of England,* writes of "the most boundless and restless faculty of soul; . . . in a moment striding from the center to the circumference of the world." [1] Edward Young in *Conjectures,* that charter of romantic liberties, tells how, "in the fairy land of fancy, genius may wander wild. . . . The wide field of nature also lies open before it, where it may range unconfined, make what discoveries it can, and sport with its infinite objects uncontrouled." Indeed, the staidest of the Augustans admired "enthusiasm," and the bold flights of original genius, although they of course wanted them checked with judgment and learning.

> 'Tis more to guide, than spur the Muse's steed,
> Restrain his fury than provoke his speed.

Dryden believed that the imagination should "have clogs tied to it lest it outrun the judgment," and Burke that "in the midst of the highest flight of fancy reason ought to preside." But they were, with reservations, in favor of its flight; even Pope

and Addison were. In a study of Young's *Conjectures,* Martin
Steinke has collected many passages illustrating the bardic
tradition in and before the eighteenth century. Or the reader
may find more and longer ones in Samuel Monk's valuable
book on *The Sublime: A Study of Critical Theories in Eighteenth Century England.* Usually the sentiments favoring
bardic wildness, if we check them with the poems their authors
admire or write, seem a little formal, uttered to justify minor,
snatched graces beyond the reach of art and the rules, or fic-
tions, tame enough, of centaurs and golden mountains, for
instance.

But by the turn of the century the reputation of the spontaneous flight of the nature-rapt mind had much improved by
certain circumstances reserved for later comment. Meanwhile,
we note only that because of these circumstances we find
trances, similar to those in which Keats' "Poet" wings away,
appearing in the works of numerous other poets. Here is one
from Leigh Hunt's "Politics and Poetics":

Oh for a seat in some poetic nook,
Just hid with trees, and sparkling with a brook,
Where through the quivering boughs the sun-beams shoot
Their arrowy diamonds upon flower and fruit,
While stealing airs come fuming o'er the stream,
And lull the fancy to a waking dream!

. . . . .

I see it now!—I pierce the fairy glade,
And feel the enclosing influence of the shade:—
A thousand forms, that sport on summer eves,
Glance through the light, and whisper in the leaves.

. . . . .

> I turn to them, and listen with fix'd eyes,
> And feel my spirits mount on winged ecstasies.

And another by Keats' good friend Reynolds, printed in the *Champion* in 1816:

> I, by meditation led,
> On the turf my limbs had spread,
> And was gazing in the skies,
> With thought-enamoured soul and eyes,
> Fancy wander'd wildly free,
> Herself amusing sportively,—
> Peopling all the paly air
> With forms fantastically fair;
> Or in fine imaginings,
> Calling forth diviner things.
>
> .   .   .   .   .   .
>
> There I lay,—by Fancy wrought
> Into most luxurious thought.

More distinctive is Keats' comment and demonstration that nature is the inspirer of myth. Hunt and subsequent commentators say that Keats took this idea from the fourth book of Wordsworth's *Excursion,*

> The lively Grecian, in a land of hills,
>
> .   .   .   .   .
>
> Could find commodious place for every god.

But the general idea that the Greeks and other primitives "saw God in clouds and heard him in the wind" is in fact again commonplace and traditional. Addison believed that the ancients felt a pleasure deeper than "ours" in poetry, "because they lived and conversed, as it were, in an enchanted region, where everything they looked on . . . gave a thousand pleasing hints to their imagination." Joseph Healy could not, as he looked upon the beauty of the woods near Shenstone's famous Leasowes, "help thinking myself surrounded . . . by those imaginary beings whom fable gave life to, skipping about me in wanton revelry." Edward Baldwin (William Godwin) in that *Pantheon* which Keats found useful marked how

> the Grecian mythology replenished all nature with invisible beings, so that whether these ancients walked in fields or gardens, whether the objects before them were a river or a wood . . . , they felt on all occasions surrounded with divine nature. . . . Their worshippers had continually present to their fancy, thin, airy and elegant forms, floating upon the winds, listening to their ejaculations, diving into their thoughts, and studious of their prosperity and happiness.

To ascribe Keats' dominant image of the Poet, rapt by the charms of nature into a wild and visionary trance pregnant of mythological lore and wisdom of the spheres, to Hunt, Wordsworth, or any specific source in literature is neither necessary nor warranted. These conventions were in the air, and had been for a hundred years. The distinctive fact with Keats is that they were not mere conventions.

THE POETIC REPORT

We get our first hints of the fact of experience vitalizing the old and respectable bardic trance in Keats when we look at his poetic accounts of specific occasions of poetrymaking. In the 1817 volume are three poems which, like the story Antonio eternally begins at the campfire—"It was a dark and stormy night . . ."—are about themselves, their own making. The first is the opening poem, "I stood tip-toe upon a little hill." We have Hunt's word for it that this poem represents a definite experience, that it was suggested to Keats "by a delightful summer's day, as he stood beside the gate that leads from the Battery on Hampstead Heath into a field by Caen Wood." The point of the poem is an ostensibly circumstantial account of a train of poetic ideas set in motion by nature. It proceeds in literal accord with the bardic formula. The poet finds himself in a hush of natural objects; the air is so still that the buds have not yet lost their dew. There is but

> A little noiseless noise among the leaves,
> Born of the very sigh that silence heaves.

Upon the form of cloud and slope the poet gazes absently, his mind passively responsive to what might be called the motor suggestions of the scene:

> To picture out the quaint, and curious bending
> Of a fresh woodland alley, never ending;
> Or by the bowery clefts, and leafy shelves,
> Guess where the jaunty streams refresh themselves.

He begins to feel a sense of elation and freedom:

> I gazed awhile, and felt as light, and free
> As though the fanning wings of Mercury
> Had played upon my heels: I was light-hearted,
> And many pleasures to my vision started.

The "posey" of luxuries which he then proceeds to pluck, that is the images of beauty which he jumbles out, are items not present to his actual sense, but mere ideas floating across his inward eye as he gazes on the generative scene around him. "Thoughts delightful came round about me," was the first-tried introduction to the series. What follows then is a running account of these thoughts given, if we take his word, as they came to his passive mind, and connected by no principle save that of chance association. First, objects of nature: May flowers, a filbert hedge, a spring with bluebells, marigolds, sweet peas "on tip-toe for a flight," a brook with minnows, staying their bodies against the current. Then, a girl with auburn hair. The maiden gives place to a tuft of evening primroses; evening brings the moon, maker of poets, which suggests surmises on the origin of myth, which leads to the tale of Psyche, to Pan, and Syrinx, to the ancient poet who, like the present one, stood in a sweet spot and fancied the story of Narcissus. Narcissus takes the mind to Diana, to rapturous speculations on her bridal night, to the faint intimations of a new myth—the love of Cynthia and Endymion bore fruit in a poet—and here on a note of admonishment and self-recall, the poem ends.

This poem pretends to be a record of fact. Its very form and quality spring from actuality, and it runs according to the bardic formula. Hushed nature is the starting point, but under the poet's musing gaze vistas open; first of other natural beauties, and then beyond gross and palpable things. Carried on the rising tide of his own free-flowing stream of thought and feeling, he reaches an intimation of the mysterious origins of poetry in primitive Greece, and floats higher, to a "truth" beyond learning's range, to a metaphor wherein poetry is said to spring from the wedding of man-in-nature (Endymion, the shepherd prince) with imagination (moonlight, the mazy enchantment of Diana).

"Sleep and Poetry," the other long poem in the volume, certainly records an actual event, a sleepless autumn night in Leigh Hunt's study. The speculations floating before the poet's eye are less simple and sensuous than those of "I stood tip-toe." The inciting event is here not a natural scene, but an atmosphere of pictures, books, and busts of poets, whence

> there came
> Thought after thought to nourish up the flame
> Within my breast.

But the process, though started by no specific physical stimulus, is the same. The poem consists of scrappy meditations given in no order save that in which they happened to occur: a series of questions, the answers to which are "sleep" and "poetry"; then an invocation to Poetry to provide the creative ecstasy according to the scheme of the dominant image:

> Yield from thy sanctuary some clear air,
> Smoothed for intoxication by the breath
> Of flowering bays, that I may die a death

Of luxury, and my young spirit follow
The morning sun-beams to the great Apollo
Like a fresh sacrifice; or, if I can bear
The o'erwhelming sweets, 'twill bring to me the fair
Visions of all places: a bowery nook
Will be elysium—an eternal book
Whence I may copy many a lovely saying
About the leaves, and flowers—about the playing
Of nymphs in woods, and fountains; and the shade
Keeping a silence round a sleeping maid;
And many a verse from so strange influence
That we must ever wonder how, and whence
It came.

The poet's own fireside is to be the starting point for this imaginary flight, whence he will wander to the enchanted grots and green hills of the mind. Notice that this poetic flight is not imagined as carrying him away from reality. Visionary truth does not exclude mastery of the world's life. He will,

> fearful from its loveliness,
> Write on my tablets all that was permitted,
> All that was for our human senses fitted.
> Then the events of this wide world I'd seize
> Like a strong giant.

A break in the text introduces the famous series of metaphors,

> Stop and consider! life is but a day.

Next, without connection, comes the pathetic wish for ten years of life, and a survey of work to be done. His poetic course will take him through realms of Flora and Pan, and at last, with a nymph of course, into the bosom of a leafy world. But at this point another question intrudes:

> And can I ever bid these joys farewell?
> Yes, I must pass them for a nobler life,
> Where I may find the agonies, the strife
> Of human hearts.

And here, to the annoyance of Amy Lowell, there emerges not an off-brushing of dreams and a prospectus of humanistic poetry, but another vision, this time of a chariot and charioteer, a mere image where she expected exposition. Then, abruptly:

> The visions all are fled—the car is fled
> Into the light of heaven, and in their stead
> A sense of real things comes doubly strong,
> And, like a muddy stream, would bear along
> My soul to nothingness.

The famous diatribe on the "School of Dolts" of the Augustan Age comes next. "But," cries the poet, not happy in the course his reverie has taken, "let me think away those times of woe," and he turns to muse on the great contemporaries, concluding with happy prophecy of the *un*-Augustan, nature-inspired poetry which he and others are to write:

> As she was wont, th' imagination
> Into the most lovely labyrinths will be gone.

As these speculations proceed, moments of high confidence are interrupted by fleeting doubts, and again the course of reverie is managed:

THE MIND'S METHOD

              For sweet relief I'll dwell
On humbler thoughts, and let this strange assay
Begun in gentleness die so away.

The humbler thoughts are then set down as they come:

                         brotherhood,
And friendliness the nurse of mutual good.
The hearty grasp that sends a pleasant sonnet
Into the brain ere one can think upon it;
The silence when some rhymes are coming out;
And when they're come, the very pleasant rout.

"Scarce can I scribble on," cries the poet, in an eruption of
delight in these fancies,
                     for lovely airs
Are fluttering round the room like doves in pairs;
Many delights of that glad day recalling,
When first my senses caught their tender falling.
And with these airs come forms of elegance
Stooping their shoulders o'er a horse's prance
Careless, and grand. . . .

       .   .   .   .   .

Thus I remember all the pleasant flow
Of words at opening a portfolio.

Things such as these are ever harbingers
To trains of peaceful images: the stirs
Of a swan's neck unseen among the rushes:
A linnet starting all about the bushes.

And, after an acknowledgment to Sleep—

                      yet I must not forget
Sleep, quiet with his poppy coronet:

> For what there may be worthy in these rhymes
> I partly owe to him—

the poem closes with a description of the spot where it was intuited.

The creative process which this poem is written to illustrate is not a nature trance, although the trance image appears in the course of it. The material and method come from night thoughts, idle turnings of the mind's pages before falling asleep; and, by Keats' statement, partly from sleep itself. But in this poem also the poet's mind, starting from a particular experience, develops a spontaneous train of thoughts, drifts along on its own current, rises to the heights of visionary "truth" (rather cryptic truth in this poem—the chariot and charioteer), and returns to earth. "Sleep and Poetry" is more realistic in tone than "I stood tip-toe"; there is in it less bardic convention and more autobiography of mind life. It is more consciously a record of drifting consciousness, though the poet intrudes several times to alter the direction of mind drift. But the kind of intellection and the means of arriving at insight are the same in both, and each presents a variety of the trance-like experience prefigured in the image of the bard.

In the "Specimen of an Induction to a Poem" a similar process is invoked, this time for narrative purpose. The "Specimen" consists mainly of an account of the images which are moving on the horizons of the poet's mind, impelling him to tell a story:

> Lo! I must tell a tale of chivalry;
> For large white plumes are dancing in mine eye.

· · · · · ·

Lo! I must tell a tale of chivalry;
For while I muse, the lance points slantingly
Athwart the morning air. . . .

. . . .

Yet must I tell a tale of chivalry:
Or wherefore comes that steed so proudly by?

The attempt concludes with a hope

To see wide plains, fair trees and lawny slope:
The morn, the eve, the light, the shade, the flowers;
Clear streams, smooth lakes, and overlooking towers.

A train of images—plumes, lances, steeds—is working in his mind, and he expects to be led along thereby to the completion of a tale. It is not surprising, that with nothing more to guide him, he should never have completed it. That he should set out with no other conductor than his mind's drift shows what faith he had in its spontaneous activity.

These three poems suggest certain probabilities regarding Keats' work-ways: First, that the dominant image of the bard symbolized a reality of his own experience; second, that he was unusually observant and interested in the free coursings of his mind, whether they appeared as flights into the empyrean, or as nature-prompted trains of image and intimation, or as slumbrous fancies of the mind's twilight; third, that he believed some kind of truth could be reached in this kind of thinking; and fourth, and most remarkable, that poetry might consist in representations, purporting to be literal, of only the shifting, random current of image and idea that makes up dreams and daydreams.

From these interests and beliefs his early poetry takes, in fact, its essential character. The motto of his first volume was two lines from Spenser,

> What more felicity can fall to creature
> Than to enjoy delight with liberty?

And liberty of the poetic mind to move by its own laws and in defiance of the laws of logic and coherence is the guiding principle of this early poetry. Of these poems it is perfectly idle to require cogency, plan, coherence, for the good reason that in them the poet is interested otherwise. This principle and these interests marked him among his contemporaries. They called him a planless, formless poet, or a bold one, according as they liked or disliked his way of writing. But they saw well that he wrote after a strange way. If it is true that Keats borrowed from Hunt and Wordsworth for his bold purchase of delight with liberty, we have a neat irony, for Hunt and Wordsworth were among those who did not approve his strangeness. Hunt confessed in a number of "The Round Table" to a penchant for order. He disliked to see even the dishes out of their proper arrangement. He chided Wordsworth in his curious and equivocal *Feast of the Poets* for nourishing "that eremitical vagueness of sensation, *that making a business of reverie,* that despair of getting to any conclusion which is the next step to melancholy, or indifference." Since "a business of reverie" is precisely what Keats makes in many of his early (and some of his later) poems, it is no wonder that Hunt also admonishes Keats for a "tendency to notice everything too indiscriminately, and without any eye to natural proportion and effect," for "giving way to every idea that came across him." These comments are in Hunt's review of Keats' 1817 volume. He makes much the same criticism in 1820, complaining of Keats' "exuberance of ideas." Wordsworth, if himself guilty of the fault, disapproved it in others. We come at this fact in a criticism of Keats' friend Reynolds, who, as it chanced, saw eye to eye with Keats regarding "wide-wandering poetry" and the trance, and practiced them according to his capacities. It will have been noticed perhaps that Reynolds' "Fairies," quoted in part a few pages back, sounds like imitated Keats (or possibly Keats was the imitator). So and more strikingly does "A Recollection":

> I stood upon the hill,
> Gazing upon the gaieties of summer,
> And banqueting my mind, with thoughts that sprung
> From flowers, and rocks, and trees. The very wind
> Could wake some feeling of delight, and whisper
> The language of its birth-place. Oh! I caught
> A silent luxury in that lone hour,
> From every thing around.

"Your fancy is too luxurious, and riots too much upon its own creations," wrote Wordsworth to this young poet of nature raptures. To Keats himself Wordsworth apparently never vouchsafed any criticism other than the graceless phrase, "a pretty piece of paganism," with which he ticketed the Hymn in *Endymion*. There is no doubt, however, that his advice would have been to order and to excise, and I think no doubt it would have been ignored.

At any rate wildness and profusion and lack of design distinguished Keats in his own day, and his contemporaries sided with or against him on this issue. George Felton Mathew, the priggish young man whom Keats once addressed as "a black-eyed swan upon the widening stream" of poetry, sided with Wordsworth and Hunt, observing in his review of Keats that "he seems to have a principle that plan and arrangement are prejudicial to poetry." One Mrs. Col. Green, a correspondent of Keats' good angel, Woodhouse, though speaking cautiously, as well she might to this sterling defender, opined that "a stranger might fancy him too wild in some of his passages."

Reynolds' position is indicated by his own practice, also by his slightly truculent defense of Keats: "Poetry," he wrote, in his review of *Endymion*, "is a thing of generalities—a wanderer among persons and things, not a pauser over one thing, or with one person. The mind of Mr. Keats, like the minds of our older poets, goes round the universe in its speculations and its dreams. It does not set itself a task." ("Poetry," Keats wrote at about the same time, "must be free! It is of the air, not of the earth, and the higher it soars, the nearer it gets to its home. . . . It knows no stop in its delight, but goeth where it listeth.") "Go on! and keep thee to thine own green way," he urged Keats in verse. Keats' publisher Ollier similarly endorsed the wildness in him:

> —Rejoic'd I see
> Thee spurn, with brow serene, the gross controul
> Of circumstance, while o'er thee visions roll
> In radiant pomp of lovely Poesy!
>
> .   .   .   .   .   .
>
> While nature's voice alone directs thy mind;
> Who bids thy speculation inward turn.[2]

Keats was obviously doing something special, and was conscious, if only by the reactions of others, of his peculiarity.

THE PROBABLE FACT

The recurrent image of the bardic trance, the purported account in certain poems of trancelike experiences of his own —nature dreams and night thoughts made poetry—the fact that many of his early poems seemed to his contemporaries, and still seem to critics nowadays, peculiarly wild and inchoate, all point to what may be called a special method of composition. The phrase, however, carries such radical implications that it is necessary to decide carefully what is meant by it.

We must notice first of all that while Keats' bardic trances and poetic reports doubtless mean something, they cannot mean precisely what they say. If we took "I stood tip-toe" literally, for example, we should have to imagine Keats standing on the verge of Caen Wood, tablet in hand, gazing with lacklustre eye upon the surroundings, and at the same time writing down with automatic speed all the ideas running in his head.

This picture, fantastic as it seems, is by no means inconceivable. Miss Gertrude Stein is said to have practiced something of the sort at one time or another, and other modern poets may be supposed to. And the practice is not peculiar to moderns. In the middle of the last century the Swedenborgian poetaster, J. J. Garth Wilkinson, whose restful obscurity Havelock Ellis disturbed not long ago by calling him the discoverer of psychoanalysis, gave this recipe for "a new method" of writing:

A theme is chosen, or written down. As soon as this is done, the first impression on the mind which succeeds the act of writing the title is the beginning of the evolution of the theme, no matter how strange or alien the word or phrase may seem.

The poem is continued by the same method, and Wilkinson found it "to lead by infallible instinct into the subject." [3] That this method led Wilkinson to doggerel proves nothing of Keats. A man whose thoughts are of oxen, as De Quincey says, will dream and make poems of oxen.

It seems unlikely, nevertheless, that Keats' interest in the freely allowed rangings of his mind materialized in quite this fashion. We know, for example, that "I stood tip-toe" was not uttered whole, on the spot, for Keats writes of finishing this song of summer in December. Furthermore, the manuscript shows much tinkering. Toward the end of "Sleep and Poetry" Keats says that he resolved to "begin these lines that very day," but by this very statement we can know that the mind drift which the poem pretends faithfully to record was not pristine and spontaneous in the writing down.

> Between the conception
> And the creation
>
> * * *
>
> Falls the Shadow.

We are concerned to know what is hidden in the shadow, for what reality of experience the dominant image and the poetic report stand.

It is, as a matter of fact, difficult to speak of a method of composition without raising the question, When is a poem composed? Common sense tells us that the sequence of events whereby perhaps a mere low stirring of consciousness, a cadence of the mind's ear, a glimpse, a faint impulse of the nerves evolves, and shapes, and finally gets to the ears of a friend or hands of a printer as a poem is an infinitely subtle and complex sequence. It includes perhaps many different varieties of consciousness and conduct from the first, fine, careless rapture to the correction of the page proof. Sometimes these events seem compacted to a discernible unity, limited in time and firmly featured. So they were when Coleridge wrote "Kubla Khan" between his waking from the laudanum dream and the call of the "visitor from Porlock." And so they were, apparently, on that autumn morning when Keats made the sonnet, "On First Looking into Chapman's Homer," in the four or five hours between dawn and late breakfast time.[4] Sometimes these sequences tend to be accompanied with a special habit of behavior. Wordsworth walked, Burns whistled, Housman took beer, and Wilkinson started writing words on a paper. Under such circumstances we can speak reasonably of at least the externals of a method of composition; and if we want to explore the internals, we have a limited area in which to look for them. But the act of composition seems rarely so clean-cut in time, or so distinct in respect to accompanying behavior, from the other events of a poet's life. In fact, if we require a temporal unity and an organic sequence of conduct for a method of composition, we shall probably have to admit that most poets write according to no method at all. More awkward still, we shall have to end our examination of Keats' way of writing with the conclusion that, since he did not make poems as he pretended, there is simply no telling how he did make them.

It is possible, however, to approach the question from another side. There is reason to believe that most poets regard a certain temper and action of the mind as peculiarly productive of poetry. Often the temper and action seem unique; so different, in fact, from all other uses of the mind that some of them refer its power to sources outside themselves. They speak of possession, inspiration, the moment of genius:

> Vous sentez un petit coup d'électricité qui vous frappe à la tête et vous saisit en même temps le cœur; voilà le moment du génie.—BUFFON

This temper and action of the mind, although it may emerge in the sequence of events leading to a poem at countless different stages, be intermittent or sustained, intense or mild, is the specifically fecund one, the energic element in the sequence, qualifying and pervading those interblended intuitings, re-memberings, composings, utterings, revisings, writings down, and rewritings that take place when time and mind and material compose to a poem. In the quality and the pervasiveness of this temper and action the method of composition consists. The question of how a poet makes poems, if it is to have any meaning and hope of answer, resolves itself, then, to the question, How specialized in the experience of the poet is this temper and action, and how pervasive?

Although the poems that we have been examining are less than literally true accounts of the events involved in their making, they can be trusted in one point. They indicate that Keats believed himself to make poetry by a highly special use of his mind. Obviously he shared the belief of his generation in "inspiration," yet with this difference from many, that he proved the experience in his own blood, familiarized it, fortified it with knowledge of the mind, and extended its modes to new and daring use.

We can see from his own and others' accounts of his habits in actual writing-down that he permitted this special temper and action of the mind to pervade the drafting stage of his poetrymaking. He wrote very rapidly. The divinity student Bailey, in whose Oxford rooms he worked at the third book of *Endymion,* reports that he

> wrote with as much regularity, and apparently with as much ease, as he wrote his letters. Indeed he quite acted up to the principle he lays down in the letter of axioms to his publisher . . . "That if poetry comes not as naturally as the leaves of a tree, it had better not come at all." This axiom he fulfilled to the letter by his own practice, *me teste,* while he composed the third Book of *Endymion,* in the same room in which I studied daily, until he completed it.

To Haydon he wrote of "things I do half at random . . . afterwards confirmed by my judgement in a dozen features of propriety." The sonnet on Burns' tomb he wrote "in a strange mood, half asleep." In 1819 he gave a full description of his method of writing to Woodhouse, who recorded faithfully as usual:

> He has repeatedly said in conversation that he never sits down to write, unless he is full of ideas, and then thoughts come about him in troops as though soliciting to be accepted and he selects. . . . The moment he feels any dearth he discontinues writing and waits for a happier moment. He is generally more troubled by re-

dundancy than by a poverty of images, and he culls what appears to him at the time the best.—He never corrects, unless perhaps a word here or there should occur to him as preferable to an expression he has already used— He is impatient of correcting and says he would rather burn the piece in question and write another or something else. "My judgement," (he says) "is as active while I am actually writing as my imagination. In fact all my faculties are strongly excited and in their full play—and shall I afterwards, when my imagination is idle, and the heat in which I wrote has gone off, sit down coldly to criticize when in possession of only one faculty what I have written when almost inspired." This fact explains the reason of the perfectness, fullness, richness and completion of most that comes from him. He has said that he has often not been aware of the beauty of some thought or expression until after he had composed and written it down— It has then struck him with astonishment and seemed rather the production of another person than his own. He has wondered how he came to hit upon it. This was the case with the description of Apollo in the 3rd book of "Hyperion." . . . It seemed to come by chance or magic—to be as it were something given to him.

Amy Lowell, with the fine feeling for the rigors of art which was characteristic of her, objects to the sentimental tone of this account and thinks that Keats was talking for effect. She insisted that he corrected and corrected. In his study of *Keats' Craftsmanship*, however, M. R. Ridley points out that practically all of these corrections were made "*currente calamo,* . . .. in the moment of composition; a word is discarded before it is even completely written, or the first lines of a stanza are written and immediately deleted." In Keats' account the emphasis is all upon speed and spontaneity. Keats was scarcely an automatic writer, but there is reason to believe that he strove to keep short the distance in mental space between conception and utterance. At times he deliberately suspended the critical function and wrote "at random" or "half asleep." He realized that in creation the intelligence (as Schiller once put it) "withdraws its watchers from the gates, while the ideas rush in pell-mell." This realization, this creative temper and use of mind, pervades the manner of his writing down.

Keats cultivated this use of the mind with some expertness of psychological technique. To demonstrate this fact and to realize the depth and vividness of his experience in composition we turn to some interesting involuntary evidence of his method.

According to the dominant image of "The Poet," and according to several of his own poetic accounts of making poems, he liked to have his "trances" lying down:

> Give me a golden pen, and let me lean
>   On heap'd up flowers, in regions clear, and far.
>
>   .   .   .   .   .   .
>
> Or, on the wavy grass outstretch'd supinely,
> Pry 'mong the stars, to strive to think divinely.
>
>   .   .   .   .   .   .
>
>   These things I thought
> While, in my face, the freshest breeze I caught.
> E'en now I'm pillow'd on a bed of flowers.

"Sleep and Poetry" was composed (in the sense stipulated) while he lay on a couch in the dark of Hunt's study. In the "Ode on Indolence" he is "cool-bedded in the flowry grass."

In "God of the Meridian" his body is "earthward-press'd." The "Epistle to Reynolds" is an account of the phantoms of a preslumbrous doze. In this characteristic attitude, the mind begins brooding on its own content. Frequently the attention is fixed on an object in a meditative stare, or by a low sound: the contours of horizon in "I stood tip-toe," the heavens in "To My Brother George," a "bright star" in the sonnet of that name. The monotonous sound of the sea or a long gaze into its depths incites other poems. He mused on the Elgin marbles, by Severn's account, for hours. But the poem, as we noticed, presently moves away from the item by which the attention is immobilized. This focus, although usually returned to in the end, is a mere starting point for the mind's voyage. On this fact Keats insists when he calls nature a book to be read, speaks of the poet's talismanic gift to call up spirits from cave, rock and fountain, and when, as we shall see, he declares that the pipers on the urn play "not to the sensual ear alone."

We need only an elementary knowledge of psychology to recognize in these details the steps leading toward unconscious cerebration, as in hypnosis or sleep. The stages, "relaxation," "immobilization of attention," "expansion of consciousness," can be found described in numerous books on the subject; readily, although in a biased context, in Charles Baudouin's *Suggestion and Autosuggestion*. Keats and the psychology laboratory agree also that accompanying this swarming of images in the mind is a heightened state of emotion.

> I gazed awhile, and felt as light, and free
> As though the fanning wings of Mercury

Had played upon my heels: I was light-hearted,
And many pleasures to my vision started.

  . . . . . .

But there are times, when those that love the bay,
Fly from all sorrowing far, far away;
 A sudden glow comes on them.

  . . . . . .

Some flowery spot, sequester'd, wild, romantic,
That often must have seen a poet frantic.

  . . . . . .

So that we feel uplifted from the world,
Walking upon the white clouds wreath'd and curl'd.

These sound, of course, like the traditional *furor poeticus,* and might be mere convention in Keats. But they were not.

Anyone who has observed the course of his own reveries knows that in really profound ones occasionally feelings of distress, even sometimes of panic and threatening chaos, crop out, and bring one wide awake again. These outcroppings of dismay are, in fact, themselves indications of the degree of liberty which the reverist has allowed his mind. Freud has this to say of the state of mind to which the psychoanalytic patient is induced:

> As may be seen, the point is to bring about a psychic state to some extent analogous . . . to the state prior to falling asleep (and indeed also to the hypnotic state). In falling asleep, the "undesired ideas" come into prominence on account of the slackening of a certain arbitrary (and certainly also critical) action, which we allow to exert an influence upon the trend of our ideas. . . . In the condition which is used for the analysis of dreams and

pathological ideas, this is purposely and arbitrarily dispensed with . . . , the undesired ideas now coming to the surface.

Keats' creative reverie often reached to this depth; he knew panic fear as well as elation in his coursings. On this point we have the evidence, not only of the often expressed feeling of terror at the metaphorical height to which the wings of bardic fury bring him—

> It is an awful mission,
> A terrible division;
> And leaves a gulph austere
> To be fill'd with worldly fear.
> Aye, when the soul is fled
> Too high above our head,
> Affrighted do we gaze
> After its airy maze,
>
>   *   *   *   *   *
>
> And is not this the cause
> Of madness?

We have not only such thoroughly conventional awareness of how wild fancy neighbors madness. There is a poem conclusive in this connection which Keats wrote while on his luckless walking tour of Scotland. It is a very factual poem, focused upon an actual recent event, and full of circumstantial detail; and it gives us a direct representation of a daydream wherein undesired ideas broke violently to the surface. It comprises a train of ideas leading not to an inspired insight of the good and fair, but to a panic apprehension. Not a good poem, it shows nevertheless how deep, how "semihypnotic" Keats' trance could be. The poem is the "Lines Written in the High-lands After a Visit to Burns's Country," and the background of events is as follows:

On July 1, 1818, Keats and his traveling mate, Charles Armitage Brown, visited the tomb of Burns in Dumfries. Keats found it not much to his mind, nor was he pleased with Scotland in general. Brown wrote in this month, "Keats has been this five hours abusing the Scotch and their country. . . . He thanks Providence he is not related to a Scot nor any-way connected with them." Brown was of Scottish descent, and this is partly fooling, of course; but a tone of discontent, probably the result of fatigue, is distinct in the first letters and poems of the Scottish tour. At Dumfries Keats wrote "in a strange mood, half asleep" the sonnet in which

> The Town, the churchyard, and the setting sun,
>   The clouds, the trees, the rounded hills all seem,
>   Though beautiful, cold—strange—as in a dream,
> I dreamed long ago, now new begun.

The sense of the remoteness of the present world and the vague, troubled sense "of having dreamed all this" are famil-iar signs of mind-weariness such as Keats was suffering.

The travelers plodded on for ten days toward Ayr and Kirk-Alloway, Burns' birthplace. By noon of the eleventh they were at Maybole, nine miles from Ayr. Here Keats made a note in his journal to Tom and began a letter to Reynolds. To Tom he mentions ruins explored, and to Reynolds he says, with a kind of resolute cheerfulness, "One of the pleasantest means of annulling self is approaching such a shrine as the Cottage of Burns—we need not think of his misery—that is all gone—bad luck to it—." But this was the morning mood. Burns' misery did not so easily pass from him. There was the nine-mile tramp to Ayr, which they came to late in the afternoon. The approach, he tells Reynolds, was "extremely fine," with rivulet, wood, and heath and the sun setting behind the black mountains of Arran, with Ailsa Crag in the foreground. There had been something terrifying in Ailsa when he first saw it: "Ailsa struck me very suddenly—really I was a little alarmed—," and they were very tired, "a few blisters, etc." The sense of moving in a dream was on Keats. "I'll not run over the ground we have passed," he wrote next day or so, "that would be merely as bad as telling a dream. . . . I endeavour'd to drink in the Prospect, that I might spin it out to you . . . I cannot recollect it." After telling of an encounter at the Burns cottage with a native tippler—"a mahogany faced old Jackass"—and some of his tipple, Keats suddenly unlocks the horde of dark shapes haunting him:

—My dear Reynolds—I cannot write about scenery and visitings—Fancy is indeed less than a present palpable reality, but it is greater than remembrance. . . . His Misery is a dead weight upon the nimbleness of one's quill—I tried to forget it—to drink Toddy without any Care—to write a merry Sonnet—it wont do—he talked with Bitches—he drank with blackguards, he was miserable—We can see horribly clear in the works of such a Man his whole life, as if we were God's spies.— What were his addresses to Jean in the latter part of his life—I should not speak so to you— . . . you are not in the same case—you are in the right path . . . —I have spoken to you against Marriage, but it was general. the Prospect in those matters has been to me so blank, that I have not been unwilling to die—I would not now, for I have inducements to Life—I must see my little Nephews in America, and I must see you marry your lovely Wife—My sensations are sometimes deadened for weeks together—but believe me I have more than once yearne'd for the time of your happiness . . . since I have felt the pleasure of loving a sister in Law. I did not think it possible to become so much attached in so short a time (178).

And now, the poem, which must be quoted in full:

There is a joy in footing slow across a silent plain
Where Patriot Battle has been fought when Glory had the
    gain;
There is a pleasure on the heath where Druids old have been,
Where Mantles grey have rustled by and swept the nettles
    green:
There is a joy in every spot, made known by times of old,
New to the feet, although the tale a hundred times be told:
There is a deeper joy than all, more solemn in the heart,
More parching to the tongue than all, of more divine a smart,
When weary feet forget themselves upon a pleasant turf,
Upon hot sand, or flinty road, or Sea shore iron scurf,
Toward the Castle or the Cot where long ago was born
One who was great through mortal days and died of fame
    unshorn.
Light He[a]ther bells may tremble then, but they are far
    away;
Woodlark may sing from sandy fern,—the Sun may hear his
    Lay;
Runnels may kiss the grass on shelves and shallows clear
But their low voices are not heard though come on travels
    drear;

Bloodred the sun may set behind black mountain peaks;
Blue tides may sluice and drench their time in Caves and
weedy creeks;
Eagles may seem to sleep wing wide upon the Air;
Ring doves may fly convuls'd across to some high cedar'd lair;
But the forgotten eye is still fast wedded to the ground—
As Palmer's that with weariness mid desert shrine hath found.
At such a time the Soul's a Child, in Childhood is the brain
Forgotten is the worldly heart—alone, it beats in vain—
Aye if a Madman could have leave to pass a healthful day,
To tell his forehead's swoon and faint when first began decay,
He might make tremble many a Man whose Spirit had gone
forth
To find a Bard's low Cradle place about the silent north.
Scanty the hour and few the steps beyond the Bourn of Care,
Beyond the sweet and bitter world—beyond it unaware;
Scanty the hour and few the steps because a longer stay
Would bar return and make a Man forget his mortal way.
O horrible! to lose the sight of well remember'd face,
Of Brother's eyes, of Sister's Brow, constant to every place;
Filling the Air as on we move with Portraiture intense
More warm than those heroic tints that fill a Painter's sense,
When Shapes of old come striding by and visages of old,
Locks shining black, hair scanty grey and passions manifold.
No, No that horror cannot be—for at the Cable's length
Man feels the gentle Anchor pull and gladdens in its
strength—
One hour half ideot he stands by mossy waterfall,
But in the very next he reads his Soul's memorial:
He reads it on the Mountain's height where chance he may
sit down
Upon rough marble diadem, that Hill's eternal crown.
Yet be the Anchor e'er so fast, room is there for a prayer
That Man may never loose his Mind on Mountains bleak
and bare;

That he may stray league after League some great Berthplace
    to find
And keep his vision clear from speck, his inward sight
    unblind.

This is a strange, an eerie poem, heavy with a melancholy
not toned and modulated to deliberate effect, but welling up
through the lines and submerging them in unintended channels of foreboding, darkening "joy" to a "divine smart"
parching to the tongue, and presently to a depression so deep
that it overwhelms "recollection" and threatens "present, palpable reality." The images of nature are darkly overcast; the
sun sets bloodily, the waters "sluice and drench" with overtones almost repellent. The flight of the ring doves is con-
vulsed. The crisis, the moment of morbid personal fear, seems
rather a deflection of the poem than a development of the
theme upon which it opens. The form of the statement is impersonal and general, the context painfully private and special.
Obviously it is a direct, an unguarded record of immediate
experience. Its authenticity is established by the letters to
Reynolds and Tom, for these record the same experience, even
to the minute details. The impression of ruins, the vain effort
to think of the mood as "pleasant self annulment," the weary
plodding, the details of scenery so grim to the mind's eye (like
a bad dream), gloomy brooding on Burns' lot, on love, and
disaster, fancy's sudden invasion of memory, and her menace
to reality itself, the barely compelled recovery in the thought
of George and Georgiana are all twice documented. Keats had,
in full fact, a bad half hour on that July afternoon.

    We can reconstruct in part the probable cluster of ideas
leading down into this vortex. In the center of the complex is

Burns, to Keats surely a symbol of the frustrate, neglected poet, "a miserable and mighty poet of the human heart," victim of a fate which might one day be his own. In the intensity of his feeling for Burns, the "partial moan" of self-identification is plain to hear. "How sad it is," he had written to Tom on the seventh, "when a luxurious imagination is obliged in self defense to deaden its delicacy in vulgarity, and not [*sic*] in things attainable that it may not have leisure to go mad after things which are not. *No Man in such matters will be content with the experience of others.*" In the sentence I have italicized, Keats and Burns are made one. Content with the experience of others is what Keats pathetically strives for in the letter to Reynolds, where also thoughts of Burns lead him to his own problems, his elsewhere confessed "Gordian knot" of prejudice and fear concerning love and marriage. Reynolds is not in the same plight ("You are in the right path"), but Keats' own prospect in these matters is "so bleak that I have not been unwilling to die." Burns drank and whored to keep from going mad. But whiskey and girls—even marriage to such as would have him—seem to Keats, as that eloquent and accidental *not* reveals, among the unattainables. "I do think better of Womankind than to suppose they care whether Mister John Keats five feet high likes them or not" (193). The alternative is terrifying. "We can see horribly clear in the works of such a man, . . . as if we *were God's spies.*" This is Lear, who has his place in the context, and carries other somber fragments. In January Keats had written the sonnet, "On Sitting Down to Read King Lear Once Again," with the lines

When through an old oak Forest I am gone,
   Let me not *wander in a barren dream* [my italics].

44

And there was the king's hard wish in Henry IV, "Let him upon the barren mountains starve." There before him were the black mountains of Arran and Ailsa, whose sudden looming had alarmed him a day or so earlier. These in part were the stuff of that deep reverie.

It began, perhaps, with an impersonal, almost cheerful content. The annulment of a self, for some days troubled and morose, in pictures of the past, grey-robed monks, and "battles long ago," was welcome anodyne. Burns and his own despair are for a while veiled in a fabric of far-off things. The daydream evolves, lulled and secured by the plod, plod of feet, moving on the track with tired, will-less regularity. Wood, water, and the flight of birds gradually recede from the inward moving gaze until they become merely bleak presences on the margins of a now concentric world. Shadows of the summer evening muffle the blue heath bells, darken the water in the hollows, and Ailsa looms over the outer regions of consciousness. The low shape of the cottage, the journey's end, emerges in remote space, and then intrudes in the dream, stirring the long latent griefs.

> But och, I backward cast my e'e
> On prospects drear!
> An' forward, tho I canna see,
> I guess an' fear!

The ruined image of Burns crowds back to the center, and close beside it, another more fearful shape—his own! The Gordian knot of love and unattainables. Farther now from the solid track, from the track of all hours leading homeward, lost in a lonely chasm, the mind bewildered shrinks and quails like a lost child, resumes indeed the child-shape. And suddenly is flooded with a surge of terror. Madness! Only a little step to that island world, not unenticing— "That way madness . . . upon the barren mountain . . . in a barren dream . . . O horrible!" But George and Georgiana, the new-married, happy lovers, who are all along strangely present among these shadows, now draw the anchor line—a gentle pull back to the world—linking memory and returning the mind to present, palpable things. The crisis is past; yet it was a fearful "gulph." One may well pray, "Oh let me not die mad, wandering in a barren dream of old and present sorrow in the frown of Ailsa, black and bare."

Infinitely richer, more various, more moving, of course, was Keats' dark current of thought that weary twilight, but the drift and burden of it perhaps somewhat as we have imagined. This unquestionable voyage of abstraction went far— to the point of terror indeed; where the latent, undesired thoughts, charged with personal fears more complex and painful, doubtless, than we can understand, exploded with ugly energy, to shatter the reverie and deform the poem recording it. The trance of this actual hour in Keats' mind-life was no flight toward the hills of vision, but a down-drifting to chasms of alarm, to another more private intimation of the truth kept closely in hidden regions of the mind.

But the striking fact is not, after all, that Keats should have a morbidly intense daydream. Many other poets and plain folk too have had the like. The significant fact is that he regarded the record of this dream as stuff for poetry, that he should allow the trance itself, set down with as much truth to fact as here evident, to compose the poem. We cannot say to what thoughtful process of excision and repair the flow of the actual event was subjected in the writing down. Certainly there is a difference between Keats' couplets and the day-dream's self. Yet the stuff and quality, even the progress of the poem, derive from the dream with a fidelity so great as to distort and mar it as a work of art. The record is literal to a fault. The evidence of this poem warrants a belief that "I stood tip-toe" and "Sleep and Poetry" may have been similarly true records of similar mental experience. And it suggests belief that Keats' method of composition, that special temper and action of the mind whereby he made poetry, was to fix upon a subject and let the mind take its willful way. Its course of wandering, wild and strange as it may be, shapes the poem, and though modified, pervades the writing down. This much we can safely say.

At times the method fails, poetic action of the mind is re-luctant and halting, the proper temper not readily achieved. The "Laurel Crown" sonnet is a case in point. Committed by a wager to write, perhaps in fifteen minutes, a sonnet on Hunt's crowning him with laurel, he cobbles out a sonnet which proves to be again an apparently true account of the mental events occurring in the allotted time.

> Minutes are flying swiftly, and as yet
>   Nothing unearthly has enticed my brain
>   Into a delphic Labyrinth—I would fain
> Catch an unmortal thought to pay the debt
> I owe to the kind Poet who has set
>   Upon my ambitious head a glorious gain.
>   Two bending laurel Sprigs—'tis nearly pain
> To be conscious of such a Coronet.

Still time is fleeting, and no dream arises
    Gorgeous as I would have it—only I see
A Trampling down of what the world most prizes.
    Turbans and Crowns, and blank regality;
And then I run into most wild surmises
    Of all the many glories that may be.

This is not a poem of the true and vivid trance. In fact, the
very point it makes is that no flight of mind took place—at
least until the very end. But it shows in this comment and
by its very dearth the kind of experience that he exploited,
and in fact required, for poetry. It is interesting because on
this occasion composition and utterance are practically simultaneous. Given the theme and fifteen minutes, what does he
do? Waits passively for something to entice his brain into a
"delphic labyrinth," to a gorgeous dream, an "immortal
thought." Nothing happens for a while, and he makes
cold rhymes on his plight. But toward the end of the period he sees something—as usual, a symbolic image—a trampling down of turbans, and crowns and blank regality. "The
laurel wreath, emblem of the poet exalted, of triumph over
crowned and turbaned heads. Hunt and Keats lofty above
kings. . . ." It is a wild surmise, taken from a little peak of
mutual admiration, and late in coming, to boot. But it is of the
proper stuff; the mind had at least started on its fecund imaginal drift.

    The sonnet "On Seeing the Elgin Marbles"—"My spirit
is too weak"—again illustrates the method.

Such dim-conceived glories of the brain
    Bring round the heart an undescribable feud.

The poem presents directly the images of this feud: mortality like heavy sleep, godlike hardship, a sick eagle looking skyward, images of terrible responsibility: the keepers of the cloudy morning winds, Grecian grandeur, time's ruins, a billowy main, a sun—a shadow of a magnitude.

It appears, also, with a difference, in "After dark vapours," which ends with a report of the imaginal content of the poet's mind under the impact of spring:

> The calmest thoughts come round us—as of leaves
> ╲ Budding,—fruit ripening in stillness,—autumn suns
> Smiling at eve upon the quiet sheaves,—
> Sweet Sappho's cheek,—a sleeping infant's breath,—
>   The gradual sand that through an hour-glass runs,—
> A woodland rivulet,—a Poet's death.

Dominant image, poetic report, and probably fact confirm and correlate to show Keats' method of composition, the temper and action of mind he found proper for poetry. It was a vivid temper, and a distinctive action of which he and others were aware. It pervades the content of the poems we have been examining, and qualified his manner of writing them down. It is more subtly present, as we shall see, in other, better poems. It is a method sanctioned largely by the psychology, and thence derived aesthetic, of the Association of Ideas.

"*I would have anyone try to fancy any taste which had never affected his palate, or frame the idea of a scent he had never smelt; and when he can do this, I will also conclude that a blind man hath ideas of colours, and a deaf man true distinct notions of sounds.*"

—JOHN LOCKE

CHAPTER TWO

THE RATIONALE
OF SENSATION

To readers who know and prize Keats' simple integrity in poetry any attempt to explain his imagination as working in consistent and submissive accord with a formal theory of mental process would be, of course, merely distressing. Certainly no such attempt is proposed in this study. Keats was surely a poet who looked not in books, but in his own heart, for the modes and materials of his art. His responses to theory were not docile and consistent, but personal and creative. Indeed, certain of the ideas to which we shall see him responding in his vivid, personal fashion were not theories at all in the sense of structures concocted and artificial, but facts of mental experience common to all men in all ages. To recognize these he needed but to glance inward. But these facts were being more widely remarked and with greater emphasis in his day, and indeed during the preceding half century than they had been theretofore. It is an emphasis which appears in philosophical doctrine, in aesthetic theory, even in casual lay intercourse. It constitutes a kind of mental atmosphere of which Keats was certainly aware, which he breathed in from many sources. And it affected his way of writing.

The facts of mental experience most talked of and written about in Keats' day and for some time before were the facts none too definitely designated in the phrase, "the association of ideas." In its popularity, in the firm grasp it seemed to provide on the mind's ways, in the swift absorption of its broad concepts and jargon into the vocabulary of the arts, even in the popular ascription of it to the invention of one man, "the association" held a place in men's thoughts closely analogous to the place of psychoanalysis in our own time.

To give anything like a detailed account of the growing interest in association, of the various contexts in which this interest emerges in philosophy, in aesthetics, and in literary practice exceeds my present purposes. A somewhat incomplete survey of the development of the association psychology has been written by H. C. Warren, but no thorough account of the influence of associationism in the theory and practice of literature has, so far as I know, been undertaken. Kenneth MacLean's study of Locke's influence, and Clarence Thorpe's *Aesthetic Theory of Thomas Hobbes* would provide good starting points for such a study. Meanwhile, by way of reminder, we may briefly rehearse certain pertinent facts.

Hobbes had emphasized the source in sensation of all ideas, and the tendency of ideas ("images" or "fancies") to recur in trains in the same order in which their sensory originals had occurred. Locke was the first to use the phrase, "the association of ideas," in describing the experiential genesis of the mind from the "tabula rasa" of the newborn infant mind. He classified ideas as "of sensation" and "of reflection," and spoke of the "composition" of simple ideas into complex ones. He drew, however, an emphatic distinction between ideas associated by virtue of a natural correspondence between them, and those joined by mere chance or custom, blaming the latter type of association as the source of much error in the mind. Berkeley divided mental content into "ideas of sense" and "ideas of imagination," and remarked the power of ideas to suggest other ideas and to combine into wholes referred to by one name and considered as one thing. Hume, sometimes regarded as the founder of the association psychology (though his chief concern was epistemological), classified the modes by which ideas are associated, reducing them finally to *resemblance* and *contiguity*. Causality, and indeed the belief in the existence of objects he pronounces to be merely associations of ideas, effected according to these two principles. Complex ideas are but unions of simple ideas. The imagination, although unlimited in its power of combining and recombining ideas furnished by the external and internal senses, cannot exceed the original stock of these ideas. In addition to these and other less noted English philosophers who concerned themselves with the association of ideas, there was the so-called Scottish school which, while it largely accepted the findings of Locke and Hume, tried to temper their severe empiricism with concepts of certain innate faculties. Also there was a continental school of associationists, of which the Frenchmen Helvetius and Condillac are representatives. In general, however, the growth of interest in association accompanied the development of English empiricism, and the association psychology is generally regarded as an English psychology.

It is, in fact, usually ascribed to the thinking of a kindly and curious Bath physician, David Hartley (1705–57), who elevated and expanded the principles of association into a great, comprehensive scheme of all human behavior, including the very purpose and meaning of life. Hartley was not an originator; his task was chiefly to extend, ramify, and illustrate the working of the associative process. But in his wide generalization of the theory, he at once implemented and illustrated the hold it had on men's minds. By Keats' time, moreover, it had become Hartley's theory, i.e., Hartley and the doctrine of association had become thoroughly associated. We shall, for this reason, examine his doctrine in some detail.

Hartley believed that any idea of anything was, in fact, many ideas about other things; that it was all a matter of vibrations, and all for the best. He had read in Locke that the irrational connections which sometimes hold ideas together might be merely "trains of motion in the animal spirits, which once set agoing continue in the same steps by which they have been used to." He had read among the queries at the end of Newton's *Optics:* "Do not the rays of light, in falling upon the bottom of the eye excite vibrations in the *tunica retina,* which vibrations being propagated along the solid fibres of the optic nerves into the brain, cause the sense of seeing?" And in his *Observations on Man, His Frame, His Duty, and His Expectations* (1749) he had expanded these two hints and others in a system magnificently comprehensive, strenuously pious (although mechanistic), and, in its elaborate machinery of mathematical demonstration, rather appalling.[5]

Mental experiences, says Hartley, are vibrations in the ether residing in the pores of the nerves and running along the nerves into the white medullary substance of the brain. A simple sensation produces a simple vibration along, for example, the optic nerve. But these simple vibrations tend to continue in miniature after the stimulus to them has been removed. (The splotch of light remains on the retina for a few seconds after the candle has been extinguished.) And when a sensation is often repeated, a type or image of itself is left more or less permanently in the mind and will "recur occasionally at long distances of time from the impression of the corresponding sensation." These vestigial and recurrent images are the elemental components of all thought.

Now when a number of sensations (e.g., warmth, whiteness, the tones of a certain voice, certain tactile sensations, etc., etc., and the sound of the word, *nurse*) are experienced repeatedly together, presently any one of these sensations (or ideas thereof) will call up the vestigial vibrations characteristic of all the others, and by frequent experience all these various simple vibrations will coalesce into a permanent undifferentiated cluster or vibratory system; and we have the relatively complex and intellectual idea "nurse." Visible and audible sensations, being the most vivid of any, tend to overwhelm the rest, hence the strongest associations will be those of the appearance of the nurse with the name, the name "nurse" with her visible appearance.

Some complex ideas, "by the number and interaction of their parts," produce vibrations equal (presumably in intensity) to those produced by sense experience. As for instance money, with its associates, shine, clink, luxury, power, happiness, etc., etc. These "exalted" vibrations thus become the intellectual affections and passions, "having the intellectual pains and pleasures for their objects." Two important corollaries attach to this proposition. First, "that some degree of spirituality is the necessary consequence of passing through

life"; since pleasures and pains become more and more associated with ideas—which in themselves give neither pleasure nor pain (works of art, bank notes, the pains and pleasures
of others). Second, since the stronger (including the numeri-
cally stronger) impressions prevail in any cluster over the
weaker, and since our sensible pleasures are more numerous
than our sensible pains, the process of association (given time)
would convert a state in which pleasure and pain are both perceived by turn, into one at last of pure pleasure. Association
has, as Hartley says, "a tendency to reduce the state of those
who have eaten of the tree of knowledge of good and evil,
back again to a paradisiacal one." This inevitable meliorism
runs through the whole fabric of Hartley's analysis. The
world, he says, is "a system of benevolences." After showing
that voluntary motions are generated by the process of association (e.g., the child, through repeated experience, associates the act of grasping his favorite toy, with the nurse's
hand in a state of contraction, with the words, "take hold,"
with the idea of a hand, particularly his own, in that state,
until that "state of mind which we may call the will to grasp
is generated, and sufficiently associated with the action to produce it instantaneously")—after proving this, Hartley goes
on to show that pleasure-getting motions are bound to be more
numerous than pain-getting ones. Man naturally avoids painful and seeks pleasurable associations. Then the pleasure-
getting ones produce, by association, new sources of pleasure.
Finally, since God is the source of all good and must at last
come to be associated with all our pleasures, the idea of God
and his goodness must at last take the place of, and absorb, all
other ideas.

The pleasures and pains Hartley sets in a hierarchy, with those of sensation in the lowest rank, followed by imagination, ambition (shame and honor), self-interest (gross and refined), sympathy, theopathy, and the moral sense. Each of these affections necessarily generates and provides matter for the ones above it. Imagination, for example, generates ambition. We desire to have others know of our riches, honors, high birth, etc. These become advantageous to us, in fact, by being made known to others. It follows that every discovery of these to others, also every mark and associate of such discovery, will, by association, raise up miniatures of privileges, pleasures, inconveniences, and evils, and thus afford, in each instance, a peculiar compound pleasure or pain, which by use of language has the word *honor* or *shame* attached to it.

Hartley's remarks on the pleasures and pains of the imagination are of the greatest interest. Most fundamental is his comment that the imagination is generated directly from sensation. The pleasures and pains of sensory experience become "transferred upon" (that is, associated with and hence made to constitute) those of the imagination. And thus, when we delight in a painted landscape, we are in fact getting our pleasure from a cluster of vestigial vibrations of good tastes, smells, sounds, pleasant eye experiences, etc., that the painting reawakens. Hartley defines the imagination as "the recurrence of ideas, especially visible and audible ones in a vivid manner, but without any regard to the order observed in past facts." In this view, as in others, Hartley was quite in the empirical tradition. "Imagination," Hobbes had written, "is nothing but decaying sense." And Addison, as MacLean points out, gives the Lockean emphasis when he says,

> By "the pleasures of the imagination" or "fancy" . . .
> I mean such as arise from visible objects, either when we
> have them actually in our view, or when we call up their
> ideas into our minds by painting, statues, descriptions, or
> any the like occasion. We cannot indeed have a single
> image in the fancy that did not make its first entrance
> through the sight.—*The Spectator,* No. 411

Nor is Hartley original in another observation, also interesting
to us, namely, of the near identity of imagination and reverie.
The process of imagination, he holds, is like that of reverie,
the only difference being that in reverie a person is more at-
tentive to his own thoughts and less disturbed by foreign objects, hence more of his ideas are deducible from association
and fewer from new impressions. "The trains of visible ideas
which accompany our thoughts, are the principal fund for
invention, both in matters of fancy and in science."

One other article of the doctrine had better be noticed here;
that is Hartley's characterization of the pleasures and pains
of the imagination as especially warm in youth. They strike
and surprise the young mind at first, but they are inevitably
superseded in our progress through life by the higher and more
exalted pleasures into whose composition they entered. This
pronouncement that the passions of the imagination must
yield, as we grow up, to those of ambition and self-interest,
sounds a little grim. And in fact Hartley was no willing friend
of the arts. "It is evident," he says puritanically, "that most
kinds of music, painting and poetry have close connections
with vice, particularly with the vices of intemperance and
lewdness." Under this interdict, the artist had to find what
comfort he could in the knowledge that, according to the sys-

tem, all subservient pains and pleasures are finally absorbed in "theopathy and the moral sense."

> Hard langage and hard matere
> Ys encombrous for to here,

says Chaucer, and fortunately we do not have to trail Hartley through all his manifold illustrations of the workings of association, although we shall have to come back presently to see what developments it produced in aesthetics. Meanwhile let us observe how widely the doctrine, as sketched by the earlier empiricists and elaborated by this father of modern psychology, pervaded literary and other kinds of thought, from the early eighteenth century on down.

The elements of "the association" are visible, as Monk has pointed out, in the earliest theory of the sublime in England, namely, in John Dennis' *The Grounds of Criticism in Poetry.* Addison, citing Descartes as authority, used it in 1712. Ideas having entered the mind at the same time, have, he writes, "a set of traces, belonging to them in the brain." When, therefore, any one of these ideas arises in the imagination, "they awaken other ideas of the same set." In 1744 Mark Akenside versified these reflections:

> For when the different images of things,
> By chance combined, have struck the attentive soul
> With deeper impulse, or, connected long,
> Have drawn her frequent eye; howe'er distinct
> The external scenes, yet oft the ideas gain
> From that conjunction an eternal tie,
> And sympathy unbroken. Let the mind
> Recall one partner of the various league;

Immediate, lo! the firm confederates rise.

. . . . . .

Such is the secret union, when we feel
A song, a flower, a name at once restore
Those long connected scenes where first they moved
The attention. . . .
      —*The Pleasures of Imagination*

The aestheticians Blair, Burke, Gerard, James Beattie, each in his own degree and fashion take cognizance of the phenomena of association. Joseph Priestley added greatly to the popularity of Hartley's psychology when, in 1775, he condensed and republished the *Observations,* leaving out the physical theory of vibrations. Erasmus Darwin expounded the principles of association for physiological purposes in *Zoonomia* (1794–96) and for the purposes of explaining the work of the imagination in *The Loves of the Plants* (1789). In 1794 Walter Whiter, an alcoholic clergyman, wrote *A Specimen of a Commentary on Shakespeare Containing . . . II An Attempt to Explain and Illustrate Various Passages, on a New Principle of Criticism, Derived from Mr. Locke's Doctrine of the Association of Ideas.* Godwin proved from Hartley that a man's morals depend on the sensations he has had (*Political Justice,* 1793). Samüel Rogers told in decorous couplets how

Lull'd in the countless chambers of the brain,
Our thoughts are link'd by many a hidden chain.

Coleridge was for a time an enthusiastic Hartleian. He came ultimately to regard the philosopher as a godless materialist (though two-thirds of Hartley's book is pointed toward "devotion"). But he named his first-born son after him, and in "Religious Musings" (1797) referred to him as

> of mortal tribes
> Wisest, he who first marked the ideal tribes
> Up the fine fibres through the sentient brain.

It has become clear, since Professor Beatty's able study of twenty years ago, that Wordsworth's entire work and life-view are fraught with the principles of association. Lamb wanted Coleridge to write a long poem on "a Five Days' Dream, which shall illustrate in sensible imagery Hartley's five motives to conduct"; and to De Quincey, Hartley's opus stood as "a monument of absolute beauty in its architectural grace . . . [having] the spotless beauty and ideal proportions of some Grecian statue."

The broad tendency of view toward art and nature fostered by these empirical and associationist theories of the mind is easy to see. Most obviously, they made men increasingly aware of the sensory origins and the large imaginal content of even the most abstract ideas. The life of the senses naturally thereby took on new importance. "Reason," said Sterne, "is, half of it, Sense"; Goldsmith declares that "the senses ever point out the way, and reflection comments upon the discovery." By the end of the century, Wordsworth was

> well pleased to recognise
> In nature and the language of the sense
> The anchor of my purest thoughts, the nurse,
> The guide, the guardian of my heart, and soul
> Of all my moral being.

This dignifying of sensations was both cause and effect of a progressive dignifying of the imaginative faculty, although here there are naturally wide individual differences visible within the tradition. Hartley himself mistrusted the imagination, and put it second lowest in his scale:

> It is evident that the pleasures of the imagination were not intended for our primary pursuit, because they are, in general, the first of our intellectual pleasures, which are generated from the sensible ones by association, come to their height early in life, and decline in old age.

It was opposed by Locke and Hume to the judgment, in the tradition of the eighteenth century, and particularly by that bitter enemy of imagination, Malebranche. Laurence Sterne, however, had rejected this dichotomy in ribald wise:

> That wit and judgement in this world never go together; inasmuch as they are two operations differing from each other as wide as east from west—So says Locke—so are farting and hiccuping, say I.

And Wordsworth and Coleridge in their different fashions put the imagination at the summit of the mind's powers.

Naturally also the devious, the fortuitous, the irrational connections between thoughts became interesting as it was increasingly understood that the elements of the mind were, in the first case, all composed by chance. Mental oddities, fears, illusions were explored and exploited. Hence Wordsworth presents the child in "We Are Seven" whose associations with death were so charmingly incomplete; hence Coleridge records magically the apparitions (if they really were so) of an opium dream. Hence both of them—by how different methods—investigate the effects of a curse. Especially reverie, close kin to imagination, took its place as a great wellspring of poetry and even assumed a kind of validity as an avenue to truth. Coleridge calls his 1797 poem "Religious Musings," and subtitles the "Mariner," "A Poet's Revery." Wordsworth speaks of the sweet dreams of daytime as "kind nature's gentlest boon," and of

> that serene and blessed mood,
> In which the affections gently lead us on,—
> Until, the breath of this corporeal frame
> And even the motion of our human blood
> Almost suspended, we are laid asleep
> In body, and become a living soul:
> While with an eye made quiet by the power
> Of harmony, and the deep power of joy,
> We see into the life of things.

Besides all these inevitable tendencies of the association there was fostered also an ever-increasing feeling for overtones and suggestions. As men became aware of the rich mesh of thought and image clustered around any well-defined experience, these remoter associates naturally assumed an interest of their own. "Desires and adorations, winged persuasions and veiled destinies" wreathed and obscured "the one supreme commandment, 'be thou clear.' "

Finally the relative and subjective nature of beauty, since it was all a matter of association, became somewhat puzzlingly apparent. To be sure, Hartley and other associationists had suggested an average or norm of association which would serve to stabilize the principles of beauty, a norm which would in respect to personal beauty, "not differ much from perfect symmetry." And the "School of Taste" found its normal and sedate standards confirmed by this kind of interpretation. But the associationist, writing on beauty, usually began by observing that some Africans must seem very attractive to other Africans, and that there can be no such thing as absolute and intrinsic beauty.

These tendencies are of the broadest and are modified by individuals according to their own bents. Sterne cavorts with his association, Shenstone solemnly dwells on its terrible force in making the child fear the birch. Akenside elucidates the part it plays in the pleasures of the imagination, Coleridge finds the pathology interesting, Wordsworth sublimates it with, perhaps, some infusion of mysticism, to the highest level of spiritual faculty. It becomes the instrument, in his system of mind, whereby the accidental and inappropriate associations clustering around a daisy or a "widow in distress" are supplanted by plain and severe apprehension of their very natures. It is the special heritage of maturity, hardly to be distinguished, in fact, from the philosophic mind, able to hear in nature the still, sad music of humanity, to feel in her a presence

Whose dwelling is the light of setting suns.

We shall speak presently of Keats and association but first, in order to understand the full implications for art of this psychology, we must glance at the work of a Scottish aesthetician, perhaps the most notable proponent of the associationist theory of beauty, wherein these implications are most completely developed. Archibald Alison's *Essays on the Nature and Principles of Taste* was first published in 1790 and by 1825 had gone through six editions. The bulk of its pages comprise illustrations of the truth that what we call the sublimity or beauty of any object in nature is never intrinsic to the object itself. Beautiful scenes, sounds, colors, works of art, etc., move us not because of their physical qualities, but always because of the ideas they suggest. The sound made by thunder, for example—which Burke would regard as intrinsically sublime—if it really were so, would still strike awe in our hearts when we knew it to be caused merely by a cart passing over a bridge. But obviously the emotions of terror, majesty, power proper to thunder are banished by the idea of cart wheels. The ideas which seem to describe and sanction Keats' mental adventures are found mainly in the first chapter of the *Essays*. There, first of all, Alison refutes Hartley by praising art and recommending the enjoyment of it. It exalts the mind, he maintains, from corporeal to intellectual pursuits. He then describes "an experience of taste" according to a sequence of events which Keats himself might have reported after writing "I stood tip-toe."

> When any object, either of sublimity or beauty, is presented to the mind, I believe every man is conscious of a train of thought being immediately awakened in his imagination, analogous to the character or expression of the original object. . . . Thus, when we feel either the beauty or sublimity of natural scenery . . . , we are conscious of a variety of images in our minds, very different from those which the objects themselves can present to the eye. Trains of pleasing or of solemn thought arise spontaneously within our minds; our hearts swell with

emotions, of which the objects before us seem to afford no adequate cause; and we are never so much satiated with delight, as when, in recalling our attention, we are unable to trace either the progress or the connexion of those thoughts, which have passed with so much rapidity through our imagination.

This awakening of a train of associations is, according to Alison, the imagination at its work. The whole nature and function of the imagination consists in this activity. Exercises of the imagination differ from other trains of thought in that they are charged, as a whole, and in each of the members of the train, with emotion. Alison describes the imaginative experience repeatedly in the early chapters:

In these, and a thousand other instances that might be produced, I believe every man of sensibility will be conscious of a variety of great or pleasing images passing with rapidity in his imagination, beyond what the scene or description immediately before him can of themselves excite. They seem often, indeed, to have but a very distant relation to the object that at first excited them; and the object itself appears only to serve as a hint to awaken the imagination, and to lead it through every analogous idea that has a place in the memory. It is then, indeed, in this powerless state of reverie, when we are carried on by our conceptions, not guiding them, that the deepest emotions of beauty or sublimity are felt; that our hearts swell with feelings which language is too weak to express. . . . When the passions are roused, their course is unrestrained; when the fancy is on the wing, its flight is unbounded, and, quitting the inanimate objects which first gave them their spring, we may be led, by thought above

thought, widely differing in degree, but still corresponding in character, till we rise from familiar subjects to the
sublimest conceptions, and are rapt in the contemplation
of whatever is great or beautiful, which we see in nature,
feel in man, or attribute to the Divinity.[6]

For the full enjoyment of beauty Alison insists that the con-
centrative and critical faculties must be driven from the feast.

> That state of mind . . . is most favorable to the emo-
> tions of taste, in which the imagination is free and un-
> embarrassed, or, in which the attention is so little
> occupied by any private or particular object of thought,
> as to leave us open to all the impressions which the ob-
> jects before us can produce.

This is true not only in our response to the beauty of nature.
The full appreciation of a work of art requires also a mind
utterly unconstrained. The effort of criticism, for example,
checks the flood of associations

> and, instead of yielding to its suggestions, we studiously
> endeavor to resist them, by fixing our attention upon
> minute and partial circumstances of the composition.
> . . . The mind, in such an employment, instead of be-
> ing at liberty to follow whatever trains of imagery the
> composition before it can excite, is either fettered to the
> consideration of some of its minute and solitary parts; or
> pauses amid the rapidity of its conceptions, to make them
> the objects of its attention and review. In these opera-
> tions accordingly, the emotion, whether of beauty or sub-
> limity, is lost; and if it is wished to be recalled, it can only
> be done by relaxing this vigour of attention, and resign-
> ing ourselves again to the natural stream of our thoughts.

For this reason youth is the period of life most favorable to the exercise of the imagination, and incidentally for the same reason, according to Alison, the young are not good critics

> because everything, in that period of life, is able to excite their imaginations, and to move their hearts . . . leading them into that fairyland in which the fancy of youth has so much delight to wander.

Such in significant part was the theory of beauty-as-association which Francis Jeffrey, author of the article on "Beauty" in the 1815 *Encyclopaedia Britannica,* freely borrowed from and described as "now universally accepted." Such was the trend of thought which prompted Hazlitt, paraphrasing Schlegel to say:

> The great difference, then, which we find between the classical and the romantic style, between ancient and modern poetry, is that the one more frequently describes things as they are interesting in themselves—and the other for the sake of the association of ideas connected with them; that the one dwells more on the immediate impressions of objects on the sense—the other on the ideas which they suggest to the imagination.—"Schlegel on the Drama"

And in a special and creative accord with this theory of beauty and this trend of thought Keats made poems.

KEATS AND ASSOCIATION

Several scholars have recognized Keats' keen psychological insights. They seem, however, to regard them as intuitive rather than informed. For example, Ridley:

> Keats indeed knew a hundred years ago as much as most of us today about the New Psychology (much of which is no more than scientifically applied common sense, and as old as the Delphic γνωθι σεαυτον), and could express himself more lucidly because he had not learned a terminology he did not understand.

Keats' naïveté has been, I think, somewhat too readily taken for granted. He was surely no man for terminologies, those flat conventions pointing toward the cool general, and away from the glow of particular events. He had a way of flavoring words; his eggs are "pullet sperm," his coachmen "Whipships," even his "abstractions" a personal kind of mentation which scholars are still trying to understand. These translations are part of his fierce knack of wringing the heart's blood from an experience, and replenishing it from his own life stream. He used this knack also at times with ideas, refreshing and changing his "source" almost beyond recognition. It is for this reason in large part that the terminology of association is not conspicuous in his writing, and for this reason that it requires a second glance to perceive the importance of association in his art.

All axioms in philosophy had, Keats said, to be proved on his pulses, but it does not at all follow therefore that there were no axioms. Traffic in ideas was not his primary pursuit; writing poetry was. On the other hand he had a quick and absorbent mind. Ideas which promised nourishment to his poetic energies, which explained the powers of the imagination, which had much to tell of the "sensorium," so active a part of his own make-up, he would hardly leave untasted. More probably he would devour and digest them so thoroughly and rapidly that they would appear in no time an undistinguishable part of himself.

The ideas about thinking and about beauty which, if we are correct, were of practical interest to Keats, which sanctioned and explained his personal experience, and set him forward in his own track were, as has been indicated, manifestations of a philosophical tendency much broader then the theory of any one man. We have examined in some detail the association psychology of Hartley because Hartley stands as a striking exponent of this tendency, and we have examined Alison's aesthetic because, as Jeffrey wrote, the associationist theory of beauty was the universally accepted one. For the same reasons we shall particularly stress resemblances between the thought and practice of Keats and the theories of these men. Whether Keats ever read Hartley or ever read Alison is a question not answerable on the basis of present knowledge, and indeed it is not a very important question. That he read many other writers in the empirical and associationist tradition, including some rather technical writers, is certain. We know, for example, that he owned Locke's *Of the Conduct of the Understanding*. He also owned, and as will later appear read, Hazlitt's *Essay on the Principles of Human Action.* . . . *To Which Are Added Some Remarks on the Systems of*

Hartley and Helvetius. He read Addison and Akenside and Wordsworth, who each in his way, reflect elements of the tradition. More important, however, than his reading or not reading any single author is the fact that Keats lived in an atmosphere of new thought about the mind and about beauty, an associationistic atmosphere blended of the thoughts of many men.

His ways of absorbing this atmosphere were also naturally many. He moved in a circle of friends who were profoundly interested in ideas, and obviously familiar with the psychological and aesthetic theories of the day. Leigh Hunt, his early idol and mentor, repeatedly used the phraseology and the concepts of association. In his "column," "The Round Table," which Keats read probably every week, for instance:

> The smallest and most insignificant thing can administer to his [the poet's] pleasure by means of association. —Nov. 5, 1815

This is a truth much insisted upon, both in theory and in practice by Wordsworth.

> The cultivation of pleasant associations is, next to health, the great secret of enjoyment. . . . By cultivating agreeable thoughts, then, we tend, like bodies in philosophy, to the greater mass of sensations rather than the less.—*The Round Table,* Nov. 12, 1815

That associations of pleasure prevail over those of pain was a specific Hartleian tenet.

> But the poet may sometimes choose to show his art in a manner more artful and appealing to more particular as-

sociations than what are shared by the world at large, as those of the classical readers, for instance.—*The Feast of the Poets*

Alison speaks precisely to the point of the effect of classical reading on one's associations with nature.

> The question [whether the nightingale is or is not melancholy] is . . . one of pure association of ideas. —*Imagination and Fancy or Selections From the English Poets,* "Milton"

Such are some of the references in Hunt. There are a number of others.

Benjamin Haydon, in *Table Talk,* defined painting as "only the means of exciting poetical and intellectual associations." The brother poet, Reynolds, exclaims in an article on the De Coverley Papers in the *Champion,* "There is nothing so pleasant as the association of ideas," and in his "Pilgrimage of Living Poets to the Stream of Castaly" he speaks of a conversation between Coleridge, Lamb, and Lloyd "on the beauties of the country, on its peaceful associations, and the purity of the domestic affections." In his *Recollections* Cowden Clarke specifically states that associations of ideas were in part the topic of a conversation between Hunt, Keats, and himself. It took place that memorable evening when "some observations having been made on the characteristic habits, and pleasant associations with the reverend denizen of the hearth, the cheerful little grasshopper of the fireside," Keats and Hunt sat down to their famous sonnet contest.

In his very creditable study, *Negative Capability* (a Harvard honors thesis), Walter Jackson Bate notes a letter from Woodhouse to Keats, which he believes refers to a conversation between these two on the association of ideas. At very least the letter shows that Woodhouse regarded the process of association as a source par excellence of poetry, and recommends it to Keats as such:

> The ideas derivable to us from our senses singly and in their various combin^{ns} with each other store the mind with endless images of natural beauty the Passions life & motion & reflection & the moral sense give adn [*for additional*] relief & harmony to this mighty world of inanimate matter.—It is in the gleaning of the highest, the truest & the sweetest of these ideas, in the orderly grouping of them, & arraying them in the garb of exquisite numbers, that Poetry may be said to consist (226).

It seems unlikely, on the basis of the foregoing, that Keats' own meditations on these matters, however free, could have been perpetually maiden. The common reference to association in the conversation of his friends, the fact that Keats was himself a party to some of these conversations made it very probable that his own casual and passing observations of the associative activity of the mind included an awareness of contemporary doctrine regarding them. We are justified in suspecting that when he acknowledges his debt to sleep for the materials of a poem, he speaks knowingly, and that when he refers to "trains of peaceful images," he is consciously using psychological terms.

These two passing comments are, of course, from "Sleep and Poetry." There are several others scattered among his

e is a merry one in a letter to Reynolds of May,
s has, after the economical fashion of the time,
oss lines on an already full page:

crossing a letter is not without its association—for
quer work leads us naturally to a Milkmaid, a Milk-
id to Hogarth Hogarth to Shakespeare Shakespear to
azlitt—Hazlitt to Shakespeare and thus by merely
pulling an apron string we set a pretty peal of Chimes at
work (143).

Keats very much liked, as will be seen, to contemplate the profound sympathy and similarity of imaginations between himself and his friends. To Reynolds he had written in March,

You, I know have long ere this taken it for granted that
I never have any speculations without assoc[i]ating
you in them, where they are of a pleasant nature, and you
know enough to [*for* of] me to tell the places where
I haunt most, so that if you think for five minutes after
having read this you will find it a long letter (115).

Hartley had observed:

If beings of the same nature, but whose affections and
passions are at present in different proportions to each
other, be exposed for an indefinite time to the same impressions and associations, all their particular differences
will at last be over ruled, and they will become perfectly
similar.

And Alison similarly pointed out how familiarity with another person's associations enabled one "very boldly to pro-
nounce whether any particular class of objects will affect him."

On the day he wrote the letter to Reynolds just quoted, Keats wrote of another aspect of association to Haydon:

It is a great Pity that People should by associating them- selves with the finest things, spoil them. Hunt has damned Hampstead and Masks and Sonnets and italian tales—Wordsworth has damned the lakes—Millman has damned the old drama (118).

On December 17, 1818, he again complains of Hunt as a negative link in an associated series. "Through him I am in- different to Mozart, I care not for white Busts—and many a glorious thing when associated with him becomes a nothing" (252).

In some remarks on his own tormented and frustrate love life, contained in a letter written to Bailey from the Scottish journey, Keats exhibits an insight into the cause and cure of prejudices, which if it were sheer intuition, would be rather re- markable. As a matter of fact, though there is none of the lingo in the passage, though Keats flushes up the pale cast of theory with his own telling words, knowledge of the principles of association of ideas is very clear to be seen. He is confessing to his "evil thoughts, malice [and] spleen" among women.

I must absolutely get over this—but how? The only way is to find the root of evil, and so cure it "with backward mutters of dissevering Power"—that is a difficult thing; for an obstinate Prejudice can seldom be produced but from a gordian complication of feelings, which must take time to unravell and care to keep unravelled. I could say a good deal about this but I will leave it in hopes of better and more worthy dispositions (193).

The Conduct blames association for all the un-
fears, prejudices, and errors to which the mind is
le tells of a gentleman cured of madness by a painful
a who ever afterwards, grateful as he was for the cure,
ot bear the sight of his physician. And Hartley de-
it to be of the utmost consequence "that the affections
passions should be analyzed into their simple and com-
nding parts, by reversing the steps of the associations
ich concur to form them."

But of course the most significant evidence of the impact
upon Keats of contemporary psychology is to be found in his
works. Certainly the *Poems* (1817) put into literal practice a
use of the imagination thoroughly sanctioned and rationalized
by the theory of the association of ideas. They illustrate consistently the aesthetic presented in Alison's *Essays*.

In the theory of association and in the criticism stemming
from it are endorsed those qualities and practices in poetry for
which Keats was conspicuous among his contemporaries. Inconsequent rambling of the mind is explained as an essential
trait of the imagination. The initial fixing upon an object of
nature, or beauty, the starting of the train of images, the be-
witching reverie, the heightened emotion, the rapt contemplation of what is good and beautiful, even the slightly dazed
return—in fact Keats' whole formula for poetry in nature—
are described, explained, and sanctioned. It would be the greatest mistake to think of Keats' experiences as preconceived, and
theoretical, because they proceed according to plan. We need
not in the slightest suspect the genuineness of these responses
to nature. Nor to art. He reacts to the Elgin marbles with
complete integrity and directness, but his report of his reac-

tion, presenting as it does those "dim conceived glories of the brain" as the heart of the matter, is a bold assumption of the sanctions for surrendering to the suggestions and keeping critical and minute attention out of the way. And so with the other patches of consciousness, which he presents as poems. They take their free, their sometimes inchoate character, directly and by necessity from the imagination. They exhibit the imagination as it works. We have seen how in Keats' mind nature leads to nymphs and mythical people and noted that something of the sort was traditional. Alison clarifies and reenforces this convention:

> In most men, at least, the first appearance of poetical imagination is at school, when their imaginations begin to be warmed by the descriptions of ancient poetry, and when they have acquired a new sense, as it were, with which they can behold the face of Nature.
>
> How different, from this period, become the sentiments with which the scenery of Nature is contemplated, by those who have any imagination! The beautiful forms of ancient mythology, with which the fancy of poets peopled every element, are now ready to appear to their minds, upon the prospect of every scene. . . . Or, if the study of modern poetry has succeeded to that of the ancient, a thousand other beautiful associations are acquired, which instead of destroying, serve easily to unite with the former, and to afford a new source of delight.

The fact that in this point of mythological associations with Nature Alison represents no unique view, but merely reformulates an idea in the air and current for a long time, reminds us of the fact that we are observing the effect on Keats of a trend of ideas, and not a single man's theory. Alison's aesthetic is highly characteristic of this trend, but as we illustrate resemblances between this aesthetic and Keats' work, we must bear in mind constantly the possibility of all degrees of indirectness in contact, and (in regard to any single point of resemblance) the possibility of a parallel rather than an indebted procedure. But, with this caveat, we are none the less justified in invoking these ideas of Alison's and other associationists where they do in fact explain peculiar traits of Keats' work; we are justified in invoking them where they help to an understanding of the poem and to a realization that Keats knew what he was about in writing as he did. The much reprehended *Poems* (1817) become, I believe, more intelligible when they are read in the light of these ideas.

These, then, are a few indications convenient to present at this point to suggest that Keats was normally conversant with the psychological theory of his time. The sources of his knowledge, precisely the pages read, the lectures heard, the conversations partaken of, we can only surmise. The details, the architectonics of the theory we may assume he left aside. The permission that the theory gave him to allow his vivid senses their rich enjoyment and to make poetry beginning with their data and wandering unreproved through the maze of associations they evoked, he seized upon eagerly. His assimilation of the theory of association was characteristically complete, and his references to it come out mainly in his own stirring idiom. But like Chaucer's Harry Bailey he too could occasionally "speke in terme."

PLAIN IMAGINATION AND FANCY

A comparison of Keats' reaction to the theory of the association of ideas with Wordsworth's will be valuable at this point, for it will make emphatically clear the intensely practical response to theory of the younger poet. Wordsworth, as everyone knows, saw natural beauty, human growth, the shepherd on the horizon indeed, the face of God, in a light derived from Hartley. He responded to the philosophical and theological implications of the association, accepting its optimism, emphasizing in his poems the by-God-arranged succession of human experience and the concept of the whole sequence as "pointing toward devotion." Of the two opposite tendencies latent in Hartley—the mechanistic and the theistic —Wordsworth constantly stressed the latter. Nevertheless, he subjected the theory to some radical alterations. For one thing, he dignified the imagination, representing it as the highest and noblest faculty of the mind. It was for him the thinking principle, whereby he could see into the heart of things, apprehend the all-wisdom of the Creator, and hear the voice of Duty, by which the heavens are kept just and strong. It is by the exercise of "plain imagination and severe" that he succeeded, as *The Prelude* tells, in freeing the objects of his young experience of fortuitous and personal associations, such as those whereby a daisy suggested a Cyclops, or a pensive nun, or a sprightly maiden, instead of the bright flower, symbol of meekness and cheerfulness, that it properly is. This is a considerably higher rating than is indicated by the doctrine of association, which, it will be recalled, places the imagination next to sensation, the lowest faculty of the mind. It involves also a distinction between the imagination and the fancy, with which none of the empiricists was much concerned.

Wordsworth also introduced the concept of the three ages of man. Hartley, in classifying mental activity as sensation, simple ideas of sensation, and complex ideas, had intimated that these three kinds of mentation are characteristic of different periods of life. This suggestion Wordsworth developed into a definite theory of three ages of man-in-nature: childhood, the age of sensation; youth, of ideas of sensation; and maturity, of complex ideas. The fancy tends to preside in youth, and the severe imagination in maturity. In "Tintern Abbey," the "Ode on Intimations of Immortality," *The Prelude,* and elsewhere, he comments on the divinely ordered progress from the child's vivid and unconscious delight in sensation, through the passionate and imaginative response of youth, to the contemplative and sensorially dim operations of the mind in maturity. For the loss of the warm senses of childhood and the rapt delight in Nature of youth, he finds ample recompense in "the years that bring the philosophic mind."

With these larger philosophic implications of the theory Keats was certainly familiar, but they do not permeate his thinking as they do Wordsworth's. His response to the doctrine of association shows chiefly in his practice in making poems rather than in any systematic interpretation of life's meaning. It is the associationist view of imagination and of the aesthetic experience that interests him, and scarcely at all its theology. He comes, as will be seen, to some conclusions on the nature of human life, but they are conclusions so integrated with the actualities of his aesthetic experience that one knows not whether to call them concepts or mere reactions to beauty. Although they stem from the aesthetic of association, they reflect not at all its piety. These matters we must explore later.

Meanwhile we can note that Keats also habitually places the very highest faith in the imagination. It was a faith not always untroubled, but he was on the whole loyal, early and late in his career, to the gift which made him a poet, "certain of . . . the truth of the Imagination and the holiness of the heart's affections." And, although unwilling to consign it to the low place of the association hierarchy—indeed, little concerned with hierarchies and schemes—he is content to keep it close to sensation. He believed that it carried him to truth by ways we shall presently try to follow, but he did not disavow its sensory origins, nor its irrational processes. He never converted its function, nor elevated it to austere theological heights. If he is a less systematic associationist than Wordsworth, he is a rather more empirical one.

Wordsworth's notion of the ages of man Keats entertained and modified, in accord with his own experience, in two notable passages. The passage from the letter to Reynolds quoted above—the one beginning with "chequer-work" and ending with "chimes"—continues as follows:

> Let them chime on while, with your patience, I will return to Wordsworth—whether or no he has an extended vision or a circumscribed grandeur—whether he is an eagle in his nest, or on the wing— And to be more explicit and to show you how tall I stand by the giant, I will put down a simile of human life as far as I now perceive it; that is, to the point to which I say we both have ar-

rived at— Well—I compare human life to a large Mansion of Many Apartments, two of which I can only describe, the doors of the rest being as yet shut upon me. The first we step into we call the infant or thoughtless Chamber, in which we remain as long as we do not think — We remain there a long while, and notwithstanding the doors of the second Chamber remain wide open, showing a bright appearance, we care not to hasten to it; but are at length imperceptibly impelled by the awakening of this thinking principle within us—we no sooner get into the second Chamber, which I shall call the Chamber of Maiden-Thought, than we become intoxicated with the light and the atmosphere, we see nothing but pleasant wonders, and think of delaying there for ever in delight: However among the effects this breathing is father of is that tremendous one of sharpening one's vision into the heart and nature of Man—of convincing one's nerves that the world is full of Misery and Heartbreak, Pain, Sickness and oppression—whereby this Chamber of Maiden Thought becomes gradually darken'd and at the same time on all sides of it many doors are set open—but all dark—all leading to dark passages— We see not the ballance of good and evil. We are in a Mist. *We* are now in that state— We feel the "burden of the Mystery," To this Point was Wordsworth come, as far as I can conceive when he wrote 'Tintern Abbey' and it seems to me that his Genius is explorative of those dark Passages. Now if we live, and go on thinking, we too shall explore them—he is a Genius and superior [to] us, in so far as he can, more than we, make discoveries, and shed a light in them— Here I must think Wordsworth is deeper than Milton— though I think it has depended more upon the general and gregarious advance of intellect, than individual greatness of Mind— From the Paradise Lost and the other Works of Milton, I hope it is not too presuming, even between ourselves to say, that his Philosophy, human and divine, may be tolerably understood by one not much advanced in years (143–144).

How Keats restamps his borrowed coin! This letter shows, in the first place, that Keats knew his association psychology well enough to understand what Wordsworth was talking about in "Tintern Abbey" (which, alas, is more than can be said for some Wordsworthians). He knew that the poem was about the ages of man and properly interpreted the brief and parenthetical reference to

> The coarser pleasures of my boyish days,
> And their glad animal movements all gone by

as denoting the child life of unconscious sensation. "The infant, or thoughtless Chamber in which we remain as long as we do not think." The associationist concept of constant propulsion of the mind upward is clear in the passage also, ". . . We are at length imperceptibly impelled by the awakening of this thinking principle," and, of course, the associationist (and Wordsworthian) view of the youthful imagination as very susceptible to all stimuli ("intoxicated with light and atmosphere"). Keats understands this orthodox sequence, and to this point accepts the theory. But he will take nothing on faith, neither the associationist's optimism nor Wordsworth's view of his own experience. Hartley has nothing to say of "Misery and Heartbreak, Pain, Sickness, and oppression"; his world is a system of benevolences, pointing toward devotion. But Keats is no devotee. The axiomatic serenity of the mature mind has not yet been proved on his pulses. Meanwhile they testify only to darkness and suffering ahead. He will speak then only of what he knows; it is the nerves which must be convinced. Curiously, he seems to doubt Wordsworth's own measure of the distance he has come. For Wordsworth implies in "Tintern Abbey" that he has already reached the levels of "theopathy and the moral sense." The passionate fancies of youth are gone. He is content to recognize the language of his former heart in the shooting lights of his young sister's eyes. The gift of the philosophic mind, last and noblest flower of sensation, is his. Its intuition of

> A motion and a spirit, that impels
> All thinking things, all objects of all thought,
> And rolls through all things

is abundant recompense for the lost joys of sensation. This is the implication of the poem; but Keats, perhaps with the bias of his own constant empiricism, will not credit Wordsworth with having so fully run the prescribed course. For though Wordsworth's "genius is explorative of the dark passages," he was, when he wrote "Tintern Abbey," like himself and Reynolds, "in a mist" and under "the burden of the mystery."

Regarding himself, at any rate, he finds as yet no confirmation of the pious optimism of a Hartley. The tragic sense of life that is in him cannot be thought away by recourse to any theory. Therefore the growth to maturity which he envisages is not so much toward serene and blessed moods, the joy of elevated thoughts, as toward intense realization of the pain of living, toward feeling "the giant misery of the world." In all this we see Keats' characteristic untheoretical response to theory, that combination of imitation and adaptation of acceptance and rejection, summing to precisely one total—himself.

In the "Four seasons" sonnet, Keats again touches the ages of man, "Four seasons fill the measure of the year." Here is rather more of Keats than of Hartley or Wordsworth. There are four seasons instead of the orthodox three, and summer, the second, the supposedly inferior age of youth—fancy—ideas-of-sensation, is in Keats' arrangement the period in which we come nearest heaven. In a rejected passage he had referred to the fact, stressed by the associationists, of the assimilation into one's own being of sensory-idealogical experience:

> He chews the honied cud of fair spring thoughts,
> Till, in his soul dissolv'd, they come to be
> Part of himself.

This is the fundamental principle of association on which, as will be seen, Keats elsewhere comments.

But the different responses of Keats and Wordsworth to the theory of the association of ideas become clearest of all in a comparison of two poems which report events of almost identical nature. Keats' poem is the one, already reviewed, which he wrote on approaching Burns' birthplace; Wordsworth's, "Strange fits of passion." It will be recalled that one of the tasks Wordsworth and Coleridge set themselves in the *Lyrical Ballads* was to investigate "how we associate ideas in a state of excitement." And in his poem Wordsworth provides

an example of such association in an experience strikingly like
the one Keats had on that afternoon of July 11, 1818.

Strange fits of passion have I known:
And I will dare to tell,
But in the Lover's ear alone,
What once to me befell.

When she I loved looked every day
Fresh as a rose in June,
I to her cottage bent my way,
Beneath an evening-moon.

Upon the moon I fixed my eye,
All over the wide lea;
With quickening pace my horse drew nigh
Those paths so dear to me.

And now we reached the orchard-plot;
And, as we climbed the hill,
The sinking moon to Lucy's cot
Came near, and nearer still.

In one of those sweet dreams I slept,
Kind Nature's gentlest boon!
And all the while my eyes I kept
On the descending moon.

My horse moved on; hoof after hoof
He raised, and never stopped:
When down behind the cottage roof,
At once, the bright moon dropped.

What fond and wayward thoughts will slide
Into a Lover's head!

"O mercy!" to myself I cried,
"If Lucy should be dead!"

This apparently simple little poem is really a rather subtle piece of psychological observation, a comment upon irrational fears and the states of mind conducive thereto. The completely unreasonable and "unconscious" nature of the lover's fear is the point of this poem. The girl, toward whose cottage he is riding, is in radiant health, her beauty each day more fresh. But, as he rides along, he falls into a daydream. His attention is lulled and focused by the bright moon, upon which his eye is all along vacantly fixed. The "hoof after hoof" beat of the horse lulls the mind to a dreamy and suggestible lassitude. The symbolic potency of the descending moon, type of ebbing life, is working on him unaware,

The wan moon is setting ayont the white wave,
And time is setting with me. O!

Ominously it tends toward the cot wherein the loved one lies, lower, and lower, half seen, until down it drops behind the black roof of the cottage. And suddenly fear explodes in the depths of the mind. "Suppose she is dead!" The parallels between Keats' and Wordsworth's poems are remarkable, but the differences between the two poets' responses to like situations are still more remarkable. Wordsworth's is a conscious, artful comment upon a psychological curiosity. Its sole point is the eruption at the end, and the point is made with utmost economy and directness. Whether it represents an actual experience in his own life, or an actuality reported to him, or a merely imagined experience, who can say? The poem is impersonalized by the dramatic device of the country lover, who naïvely regards the incident as one all lovers will understand. This is the typical Wordsworthian peasant, in whom the passions may be observed in their uncorrupted simplicity. The psychological, the romantic, and the dramatic values of the situation are all neatly organized in an act of creation wholly different in quality from the event described.

Keats' poem, as we have seen, is of the raw stuff of actuality. His rather feeble effort to impersonalize merely blurs the effect of the poem. It wanders somewhat in its course; and its design, or lack of design, is determined by the chance dynamic of the real event. Keats' attitude toward the experience as a whole is equivocal and uncertain. It is, in other words, not nearly so good a poem as Wordsworth's precisely because it is so faithful to the actual structure of the event described. The train of images, the arbitrary and chance course of the mind on that afternoon, was not for him merely the raw stuff of a possible poem; it was the very act of imagination, "decaying sensation" which, according to Keats' light, must be the substance of the poem. Put side by side, these poems provide a nice example in the advantage of "emotion recollected in tranquillity" over the "Delphic labyrinth," of art over surrender to the mind's flow.

Wordsworth's artful reconstruction in this "Lucy poem" of an event which took place actually in the uncultivated and inchoate regions of the mind, and his division and theologizing of the imagination indicate at all events a use of association much more abstract and intellectual than Keats'. In this instance it proved the more profitable use. But fortunately it is not always so. The immediacy, and the nearness to the mind stream which confuse "Lines Written in the Highlands" and make "I stood tip-toe" bewildering, work to exquisite effect in other poems. For Keats ultimately learned, not to mistrust and supplant his sensuous imagination, but to discover in its energies a principle of form, telling in art and, as he believed, eloquent of the very nature of experience.

*"Mein Freund, das grad' ist Dichter's Werk
Dass er sein Träumen deut' und merk'."*

—HANS SACHS in *Die Meistersinger*

CHAPTER THREE ❦

ENDYMION:
THE TECHNIQUE
OF THE DREAM

K<small>EATS</small>' hypnotic and associational way of making poetry is naturally most evident in his lyric poems, since that genre most readily permits spontaneous overflowings of the mind. It might be said, in fact, that in these poems Keats is merely carrying a traditional license to new lengths. But the method is visible also in the long narrative *Endymion.* An understanding of how Keats' psychological interest and shaping principles prevailed in the making of this poem may possibly clear up some of the abundant confusion for which the criticism of it has been notable.

One approaches *Endymion,* indeed, with misgivings. It is a perilous jungle, a tangled overgrowth of luxuriant fancy, serenely beautiful in certain regions, lush and stifling elsewhere, counter-crossed by broken trails of event, haunted by vague symbols and half-shaped meanings. It breathes an atmosphere conducive to luminous half thoughts and starry speculations, delightful to the fresh-minded reader and generally alarming to scholars,

> the unimaginable lodge
> For solitary thinkings; such as dodge
> Conception to the very bourne of heaven,
> Then leave the naked brain.

Scholarship's resolve to let nothing dodge conception, if it can catch it, its maiden aversion to mental nakedness are conspicuous in the criticism of this poem, for it has required of *Endymion* a message. Although Keats' contemporaries and readers for sixty years after seem to have been willing to take it merely as a wild and luxuriant tale, later criticism would enhance its heady wine with a bush of allegory—in fact, a whole thicket. To this process some highly distinguished minds have contributed, with whom it would be rash to differ were it not that they already differ eagerly with one another. There is added comfort, too, in the fact that some others, equally distinguished, find in the poem no allegory at all. No doubt the problem is mainly one of terms. Allegory by its nature usually asks some degree of interpretation on the part of the reader. The *significatio* of the middle ages made all clear, but it is long gone out of use. Even Spenser left to the reader some leeway for individual understanding. Yet if the term allegory is to keep a meaning, an allegory should provide a reasonable degree of certainty in its significations and not leave every man his own allegorist. And to the question, What does *Endymion* signify? there have been a distressing number of different answers. "Let the allegory alone," growled Hazlitt to carping readers of *The Faerie Queene,* "the allegory won't bite you." There is something to be said for letting alone an allegory which bites in so many different places. Certainly there are in this poem animate symbols of Keats' mental life.

Who can doubt the symbolic reference in Book IV, where Endymion with his Indian Maid—both sleeping on sleeping, winged steeds—dreams he is in the courts of heaven, and wakes to find his dream come true. We should recognize in this flight one of Keats' voyages of the imagination even had he not written to Bailey in November, 1817, "The Imagination may be compared to Adam's dream—he woke and found it truth." With this clue, the critical mind which, as Keats put it, "prefers a truth to an eagle," and likes not "a sketchy intellectual landscape," can go far. It cannot, I think, rightly use this or any of the other clues in this poem to wind through the whole forest. Whatever *Endymion* is, it is not what Finney calls it, an allegory "carefully planned in advance, with episodes invented and arranged in four groups before a single word was written," of the Platonic quest for immortality.

We may as well avoid a long argument on this point and set down merely these facts:

1) Keats refers to that passage wherein Finney sees an explicit statement of the Platonic philosophy of beauty as a very personal utterance, not logical in its sequence, and probably quite incomprehensible to his learned publisher, Taylor. This seems an odd way to speak of a statement of so intelligible and familiar a doctrine as Platonism:

> The whole thing must I think have appeared to you, who are a consequitive [*sic*] Man, as a thing almost of mere words—but I assure you that when I wrote it it was a regular stepping of the Imagination towards a Truth. My having written that Passage Agreement will perhaps be of the greatest Service to me of any thing I

ever did. It set before me at once the gradations of Happiness even like a kind of Pleasure Thermometer—and is my first Step towards the chief attempt in the Drama —the playing of different Natures with Joy and Sorrow (91).

2) Benjamin Bailey, with whom Keats lived some weeks while *Endymion* was in the writing and with whom, as we know, he talked poetry and philosophy, writes as follows of the "second fault" of *Endymion:*

> The approaching inclination it has to that abominable principle of Shelley!—that sensual love is the principle of things. Of this I believe him to be unconscious, and can see how by process of the imagination he might arrive at so false delusive and dangerous conclusion.

The Neo-Platonism ascribed to Keats certainly involves the "abominable" principle. However, a conclusion arrived at unconsciously, and never discussed with Bailey, would hardly have been the point of a planned allegory.

3) If we choose to call *Endymion* an allegory, it follows that the hero's long wanderings in quest of his love must be taken as educative, as a series of graduated tests preparing him for immortality—or something else high. So, in fact, the allegorizing critics take it. But the sufficient reason for the long deferment of his hopes is given several times in the poem, namely, the natural shyness of the virgin Diana to acknowledge that Eros has triumphed over her. At the end of the poem, to be sure, with the prodigality and ill-logic of a true goddess, she adds several more reasons, among them one that suggests the "test theme," but the lines appear to be mere care-

less rationalization, ex post facto, of the series of unreasonable events which compose the poem.

"A Man's life of any worth," said Keats, "is a continuall allegory," and in this sense Endymion's is one also. Events and characters assume and put off symbolic meaning in the course of this beautiful and chaotic and characteristic tale. It can be read as an intermittent parable of love and beauty. But the allegorical elements in the poem, like all the other elements, are in the shape of wildly suggestive intimations, not in a consistent scheme. To attempt to bring these to a single focus, to make of them an articulate whole, to speak of stages of discipline and of philosophic systems as the meaning of *Endymion* is to force facts and ignore contradictions, to miss, indeed, the spirit of the poem and the interesting light it throws on Keats' way of making poetry.

For *Endymion* is significant mainly of a philosophy of composition, an interesting and unique development of the philosophy which produced "I stood tip-toe," "Sleep and Poetry," and the other trancelike poems we have considered. The essense of it is spontaneity, liberty of the mind, a fidelity as close as may be to the hardly channeled current of thoughts, whose flood constitutes the sensuous imagination of association aesthetics. Only this time the poem takes what is perhaps its essential form and quality, not from the trance in Nature nor the waking reverie, but from the shape and texture of the dream. Obviously this is not to say that Keats composed it in his sleep, nor even that he dreamed the general content of the poem. It means merely that he saw in the mind's life-in-dream a particularly pure and vivid variety of the creative imagination, and that he allowed the cloudy imprint of this variety to impress his poem.

How little he planned it in advance, at any rate, we have the best possible way of knowing, namely, his own accounts. These all point away from plan and preconception to that reliance upon the impulse of the thought stream so characteristic of him. They are rather rueful in tone, for the conduct of the thought stream in *Endymion* did not satisfy him. His sense, in retrospect, of the inadequacy of this poem was indeed troubling to his faith in the sensuous imagination. In the first Preface, which he was, happily, persuaded not to publish, he says frankly that when he began he had no inward feel of being able to finish, "and as I proceeded my footsteps were all uncertain." To Bailey he announced that the poem "will be a test, a trial of my Powers of Imagination and chiefly of my invention which is a rare thing indeed—by which I must make 4000 lines of one bare circumstance. . . ." To Haydon, that the "one great contrast" between *Endymion* and "Hyperion" will be that the hero of *Endymion* "being mortal is led on, like Buonaparte, by circumstance; whereas the Apollo in Hyperion being a fore-seeing God will shape his actions like one." To Hessey, that the slipshod *Endymion* was "written independently *without Judgement,*" and finally to Shelley, that when he wrote *Endymion* his mind was "like a pack of scattered cards." These deprecations are interesting in several ways, but the present point is that they indicate an original unpremeditation and a truancy of "judgement" which in retrospect seemed slipshod.

And with this verdict, his contemporaries, friend and foe, completely agreed. The hard-pated politician, John Wilson

Croker, made the point in one of his unpleasantries; Keats, he professes to believe, is merely amusing himself in *Endymion* with the game of *bouts rimés,* "but, if we recollect rightly, it is an indispensable condition of this play that the rhymes, when filled up, shall have a meaning. . . . Our author has no meaning." Jeffrey speaks more kindly to the same effect:

> his [ornaments and images] . . . are poured out without measure or restraint, and with no apparent design but to unburden the breast of the author, and give vent to the overflowing vein of his fancy. The thin and scanty tissue of his story is merely the light framework on which his florid wreaths are suspended; and while his imaginations go rambling and entangling themselves every where, like wild honeysuckles, all idea of sober reason, and plan, and consistency, is utterly forgotten, and "strangled in their waste fertility."

Shelley complained, in that good interchange of artists' frankness, wherein biographers perversely hear a miffy tone, of the indistinct profusion with which the treasures of *Endymion* were outpoured. Even the ever-approving Hunt, hearing "that I was getting on to the completion of 4000 lines, Ah! says Hunt, had it not been for me they would have been 7000."

Here is the old complaint which we have heard of the *Poems.* Wildness, formlessness, redundancy. To those happy men who knew and loved Keats, and to those who did not, the point for remark in *Endymion,* like the *Poems,* is not allegory and meaning, but the method, or as they mistook, the unmethod of its composition. And the complaint persists in later criticism. "He seems at times to be thinking aloud," remarks

Lord Houghton; "There are no complete conceptions, no continuance of adequate words," objects Bagehot; and Notcutt observes, "Taken simply, it has the incoherence of a broken dream," and himself proceeds to take it any way *but* simply. All this complaint, whether just or not, is natural. For Keats is writing with his eye not upon a form and a plan, but upon a special kind of imaginative activity, illustrated and sanctioned by the pervasive association psychology. Hence he is accused of lack of judgment. It is a case truly rather of error than of lack. For while the profusion of images and associations, which makes *Endymion* (what Keats called it) "a feverish attempt," may have been the result of an imperfect aesthetic, it was certainly not the result of ignorance of the virtue of form in art. The incoherence of a broken dream is not accidental.

IMAGES AND EXPONENTS

We cannot hope closely to follow all the fluxes and refluxes of Keats' excited mind as he allowed *Endymion* to emerge and shape itself through the spring and summer of 1817. But we can note certain passages which show that in writing the poem his thought was hovering around the problems of the mind and the fashion in which it assimilates and associates sensation. Even Francis Jeffrey was aware of this interest in the poem, and praised the feeling it showed of "those mysterious relations by which visible and external things are assimilated with inward thoughts and emotions, and become the images and exponents of all thoughts and passions." These relations are,

of course, the very focus and subject of the theory of the association of ideas, and they are certainly an important part of
Endymion.

The opening lines of the poem are famously beautiful.
They are also technically psychological, a fact usually overlooked.

> A thing of beauty is a joy forever:
> Its loveliness increases.

According to friend Stephens the opening came to the poet
first as,

> A thing of beauty is a constant joy.

However phrased, it is the continuously waxing power of
beauty through recollection, of which Keats goes on to speak,
a topic interesting also to Wordsworth, and indeed to all of
the associationists. And why increases? The answer lies in the
essential principles of association. For in this system, pleasurable associations ever prevail over painful ones, and beauty becomes more beautiful in retrospect, through constantly in-
creasing associations. For example, in music, according to
Hartley, the concords formed from the twelve semitones in
the octave are more in number than the discords, and the
harshness of the last passes by degrees into the limits of pleasure. "If there be [in landscape beauties] a precipice, a cataract,
a mountain of snow, &c in one part of the scene, the nascent
ideas of fear and horror magnify and enliven all the other ideas,
and by degrees pass into pleasures by suggesting security from
pain."

Accordingly Payne Knight in his *Analytical Inquiry into
the Principles of Taste* (1805) writes:

As all pleasures of the intellect arise from the association of ideas, the more the materials of association are multiplied, the more will the sphere of these pleasures be enlarged. To a mind richly stored almost every object of nature or art that presents itself to the senses either excites fresh trains and combinations of ideas, or vivifies and strengthens those which existed before, so that recollection enhances enjoyment, and enjoyment brightens recollection.

This is not Keats' language and it seems a texture very remote from the quiet loveliness of the first lines of *Endymion*. Yet in the famous passage on the imagination in the most famous letter to Bailey he discusses in his own warm, personal words just this phenomenon:

The simple imaginative Mind may have its rewards in the repeti[ti]on of its own silent Working coming continually on the Spirit with a fine Suddenness—to compare great things with small—have you never by being Surprised with an old Melody—in a delicious place—by a delicious voice, fe[l]t over again your very Speculations and Surmises at the time it first operated on your Soul—do you not remember forming to yourself the singer's face more beautiful that [*for* than] it was possible and yet with the elevation of the Moment you did not think so—even then you were mounted on the Wings of Imagination (68).

That is Keats, and it bears the unmistakable accent of his voice. But it is not the sheer intuition of the young genius, ignorant of the psychology of his time. In one of the *Essays:*

On Poetry and Music by James Beattie, of whose stodgy verse Keats was at one time fond, there occurs this passage:

> I hinted at the power of accidental association in giv-
> ing significancy to musical compositions. It may be re-
> marked further, that association contributes greatly to
> heighten their agreeable effect. We have heard them per-
> formed, some time or other, in an agreeable place per-
> haps, or by an agreeable person, or accompanied with
> words that describe agreeable ideas; or we have heard
> them in our early years; a period of life, which we seldom
> look back upon without pleasure, and of which Bacon
> recommends the frequent recollection as an expedient to
> preserve health. Nor is it necessary, that such melodies
> or harmonies should have much intrinsic merit, or that
> they should call up any distinct remembrance of the
> agreeable ideas associated with them. There are seasons,
> at which we are gratified with very moderate excellence.
> In childhood, every tune is delightful to a musical ear;
> in our advanced years, an indifferent tune will please,
> when set off by the amiable qualities of the performer,
> or by any other agreeable circumstance.—During the
> last war, the *Belleisle march* was long a general favourite.
> It filled the minds of our people with magnificent ideas
> of armies, and conquest, and military splendor; for they
> believed it to be the tune that was played by the French
> garrison when it marched out with the honours of war,
> and surrendered that fortress to the British troops.—The
> flute of a shepherd, heard at a distance, in a fine summer
> day, amidst a beautiful scene of groves, hills, and waters,
> will give rapture to the ear of the wanderer, though the
> tune, the instrument, and the musician, be such as he
> could not endure in any other place.—If a song, or piece

of music, should call up only a faint remembrance, that we were happy the last time we heard it, nothing more would be needful to make us listen to it again with peculiar satisfaction (Part I, Chap. VI).

This last is a patch of the classic association-texture, and Alison quite naturally fits it into his own fabric. In his first chapter, the point of which is to show that an increased exercise of the imagination—in other words an increase of associations—increases the beauty of any object, Alison writes:

> The influence of such associations, in increasing either the beauty or sublimity of Musical composition, can hardly have escaped any person's observation. The trifling tune called Belleisle March is said, by a very eminent writer, to have owed its popularity among the people of England, to the supposition, that it was the tune which was played, when the English army marched into Belleisle, and to its consequent association with images of fame, and conquest, and military glory.

Keats' remarks are obviously close in tenor, to some extent even in phrase, to Beattie's; on the other hand, he agrees with Alison in calling the enhancing process of association a function of the imagination. But whether he had read one or both of these is not the essential point. The point is that in his letter to Bailey he is speaking in good set terms, and with the traditional illustration of the power of associations, and of the identity of these with imagination. It is this psychological fact to which the line in *Endymion* refers, and on which the next lines enlarge:

It will never
Pass into nothingness; but still will keep
A bower quiet for us, and a sleep
Full of sweet dreams, and health, and quiet breathing.

We put off consideration of these important lines for the present and go on:

Therefore, on every morrow, are we wreathing
A flowery band to bind us to the earth.

This, obviously, is the unbroken path along which, by the process of association, impressions of eye, ear, palate, etc., are climbing in endless procession upward to form the essential being of men. With Wordsworth it became the tie of natural piety which, woven of the rainbow, of daffodils, of the songs of Highland girls, bound his days each to each; those spots of time, with renovating virtue—the stone, the withered leaf, the spangled heavens

Which spake perpetual logic to my soul,
And by an unrelenting agency
Did bind my feelings even as in a chain.

And it may be that for the idea here expressed of the diurnal harvest of sensations, which constantly bind the spirit of man to the earth which shapes it, Keats is immediately in debt to Wordsworth. But behind both Keats' and Wordsworth's experience is the common matrix of association. Alison, like Wordsworth, had given it the moral, Hartleian stress:

Whether in the scenery of nature, amid the works and
inventions of men, amid the affections of home, or in

the intercourse of general society, the material forms which surround us are secretly but incessantly influencing our character and dispositions. And in the hours of the most innocent delight, while we are conscious of nothing but the pleasures we enjoy, the beneficence of Him that made us, is employed in conducting a secret discipline, by which our moral improvement is consulted.

Keats' poem continues:

> Such the sun, the moon,
> Trees old, and young sprouting a shady boon
> For simple sheep; and such are daffodils
> With the green world they live in; and clear rills
> That for themselves a cooling covert make
> 'Gainst the hot season; the mid forest brake,
> Rich with a sprinkling of fair musk-rose blooms:
> And such too is the grandeur of the dooms
> We have imagined for the mighty dead;
> All lovely tales that we have heard or read:
> An endless fountain of immortal drink,
> Pouring unto us from the heaven's brink.

These are, of course, the pleasures of sense, and the pleasures of the imagination, the basis—in this order—of all other affections and passions. Above them loom the more austere and unreproved pleasures of ambition, self-interest, sympathy, theopathy, and the moral sense. Of these Keats, whose young life was dedicated to the truth of the imagination, could not, or at least would not, for himself speak. However, I think it is possible that he hints at them in the famous pleasure thermometer at the end of Book I, which Finney and other allegorizing readers believe holds the key to the whole poem, and indicates the stages, love of nature, love of art, friendship, and love, alleged to be Neo-Platonic. We must leap over some intervening lines to examine it.

> Wherein lies happiness? In that which becks
> Our ready minds to fellowship divine,
> A fellowship with essence; till we shine,
> Full alchemiz'd, and free of space. Behold
> The clear religion of heaven! Fold
> A rose leaf round thy finger's taperness,
> And soothe thy lips: hist, when the airy stress
> Of music's kiss impregnates the free winds,
> And with a sympathetic touch unbinds
> Eolian magic from their lucid wombs:
> Then old songs waken from enclouded tombs;
> Old ditties sigh above their father's grave;
> Ghosts of melodious prophecyings rave
> Round every spot where trod Apollo's foot;
> Bronze clarions awake, and faintly bruit,
> Where long ago a Giant Battle was;
> And, from the turf, a lullaby doth pass
> In every place where infant Orpheus slept.
> Feel we these things?——that moment have we stept
> Into a sort of oneness, and our state
> Is like a floating spirit's.

Here again are sensation and imagination, with a very Keatsian and a very associationist comment on the close relationship between them. Endymion continues:

> But there are
> Richer entanglements, enthralments far
> More self-destroying, leading, by degrees,

To the chief intensity: the crown of these
Is made of love and friendship.

That, as Hamlet says, would be scanned. What is the point, in this context, of "self-destroying"? If it is meant to re-enforce the lines about stepping into a oneness and the state like a floating spirit's, it seems a little oblique. Let us also note the reference of *these*. They are the entanglements which *lead to*, but do not, according to the literal words, *constitute* the chief intensity. The crown of these entanglements is, we are told, love. We can, of course, arbitrarily decide that what Keats intended to say is that love is the chief intensity. What the words say is that love is the crown of a series leading to the chief intensity:

> The crown of these
> Is made of love and friendship, and sits high
> Upon the forehead of humanity.
> All its more ponderous and bulky worth
> Is friendship, whence there ever issues forth
> A steady splendour; but at the tip-top,
> There hangs by unseen film, an orbed drop
> Of light, and that is love.

This certainly sounds like something climactic, and the allegorists, many of them, therefore regard the stage of love as, in Keats' dark conceit, the *summum bonum* of existence. But Endymion himself says presently that by this love he means the mere commingling of passionate breath, that he is talking about something even higher than this apex. For he is "one who keeps within his steadfast aim, a love immortal," the love of Cynthia, goddess of the moon. Meanwhile, to continue where we broke off, there follow some remarks emphasizing the profound assimilation into one's being of the experience of love:

> Its influence,
> Thrown in our eyes, genders a novel sense,
> At which we start and fret; till in the end,
> Melting into its radiance, we blend,
> Mingle, and so become a part of it,—
> Nor with aught else can our souls interknit
> So wingedly: when we combine therewith,
> Life's self is nourish'd by its proper pith,
> And we are nurtured like a pelican brood.

The force of all experience is constantly cumulative; pleasures and pains of all sorts are reinforced and intensified by those impressions of former pleasures and pains which are stored in the mind and come flooding in on new kindred experience. Life's self, by the laws of association, is ever nourished by its proper pith. And now there follow some lines on the power of love to overcome ambition:

> Aye, so delicious is the unsating food,
> That men, who might have tower'd in the van
> Of all the congregated world, to fan
> And winnow from the coming step of time
> All chaff of custom, wipe away all slime
> Left by men-slugs and human serpentry,
> Have been content to let occasion die,
> Whilst they did sleep in love's elysium.

Perhaps the only thing of which we can be certain in this strange and equivocal passage is that it is intended to describe some sort of hierarchy. The stages of experience which it suggests are surely not precisely four Platonic ones; for there are at least five of them. As we have seen, Keats referred to these lines as if they were the toil of his own brain. I think we can believe him; that we may reasonably suspect in them his own inveterate accent working on a scale that was originally the seven stages of Hartleian associationism. Sensation and imagination are there. Of that there is no doubt. In the classic scheme ambition and self-interest come next above, and in Keats' hierarchy, at this point comes the slightly intrusive notion of "self-destroying" enthralments. At the top of these is friendship and love. These are of course included in the pleasures and pains of sympathy in the Hartley categories; they are generated by, and so inevitably displace, self-interest and ambition. Accordingly Endymion's reflections turn to those men content to let occasion die for the pleasures of love. Two of the Hartleian stages are still unaccounted for—theopathy, and the moral sense. Theopathy, as a matter of fact, is precisely Endymion's trouble, but it is most emphatically not the theopathy Hartley had in mind. The love of a goddess

> With such a paradise of lips and eyes,
> Blush tinted cheeks, half smiles, and faintest sighs.

This is Keats' version of theopathy. And what, in this series, does it mean? If we turn back to "I stood tip-toe" we find grounds for a good guess. That poem also was concerned with the love of Endymion and Cynthia, and Keats called it originally "My Endymion." At the very end of it, we saw emerging the outlines of a myth. The shepherd-man-in-nature in union with moonlight begets poetry. Moonlight is obviously the world of enchantment, the world of the imagination. And so Keats places on Hartley's (and Wordsworth's) God-loving summits a citadel nearer to his own heart's desire, the poet's imagination. It isn't at all logical, of course, for he has already put the imagination down where it belongs, next to sensation. But it is Keats.

These are speculations, perhaps, of that spacious sort to which the cloudy symbols of this high romance beguile one. We must not claim for them more than they are worth. Nothing could be farther from the truth than to conceive Keats as in this passage simply versifying Hartley's seven stages; and nothing is farther from the present intention than to suggest a new allegory for this be-allegorized poem. We might better use Keats' phrase again, and call the passage "an isolated verisimilitude." On the other hand, Keats set store by the lines. They cleared up, by his own account, certain ere-while confused matters in his mind. It seems a reasonable guess that they represent a revision of the associationist series of pleasures and pains, a revision which placed the imagination paradoxically near the low level of sensation, and put it again at the summit where, for Hartley, God was.

To return to the opening lines:

> Nor do we merely feel these essences
> For one short hour; no, even as the trees
> That whisper round a temple become soon
> Dear as the temple's self, so does the moon,
> The passion poesy, glories infinite,
> Haunt us till they become a cheering light
> Unto our souls, and bound to us so fast,
> That, whether there be shine, or gloom o'ercast,
> They alway must be with us, or we die.

Again, the association of sensation into the spiritual being: "those mysterious relations by which visible and external things are assimilated with inward thoughts and emotions, and become the images and exponents of all thoughts and passions." This is the content that interested Jeffrey. This was the quality which Keats' friend Reynolds found interesting in their common idol Chaucer, "the clear and breathing poet of the months of April and May—of morning—of meadows— of birds and their harbours—of internal feelings as connected with external nature." It was, in fact, the interest of the age, the phenomenon of association of ideas; and when Keats exclaims in the opening lines of *Endymion* on the increase of beauty, on the sensory ties which bind us to the earth, when he places the pleasures of the imagination generically close to those of the senses, when, if our suspicion is right, he reviews and revises the seven classes of pleasures, he is reflecting these interests and thinking in the current idiom.

There is but one more strand of connection to be noted. On Feb. 4, 1818, a year after *Endymion* was completed, William Hazlitt delivered at the Royal Institution a lecture on Thomson, Cowper, and Crabbe. Keats attended, and wrote his brother that Hazlitt "praised Cowper and Thomson, but gave Crabbe an unmerciful licking." He must have recognized his own strain of thought of the spring before when he heard:

> We become attached to the most common and familiar images, as to the face of a friend whom we have long known, and from whom we have received many benefits. It is because natural objects have been associated with the sports of our childhood, with air and exercise, with

our feelings in solitude, when the mind takes the strongest hold of things, and clings with the fondest interest to whatever strikes its attention; with change of place, the pursuit of new scenes, and thoughts of distant friends; it is because they have surrounded us in almost all situations, in joy and in sorrow, in pleasure and in pain; because they have been one chief source and nourishment of our feelings, and a part of our being, that we love them as we do ourselves.

There is, generally speaking, the same foundation for our love of Nature as for all our habitual attachments, namely, association of ideas. But this is not all. That which distinguishes this attachment from others is the transferable nature of our feelings with respect to physical objects; the associations connected with any one object extending to the whole class. . . . If we have once associated strong feelings of delight with the objects of natural scenery, the tie becomes indissoluble, and we shall ever after feel the same attachment to other objects of the same sort. . . . The greatest number and variety of physical objects do not puzzle the will, or distract the attention, but are massed together under one uniform and harmonious feeling. The heart reposes in greater security on the immensity of Nature's works, "expatiates freely there," and finds elbow room and breathing space. We are always at home with Nature. . . . If we have once enjoyed the cool shade of a tree, and been lulled into a deep repose by the sound of a brook running at its foot, we are sure that wherever we can find a shady stream, we can enjoy the same pleasure again; so that when we imagine these objects, we can easily form a mystic personification of the friendly power that inhabits them, Dryad or Naiad, offering its cool fountain or its tempting shade. Hence the origin of the Grecian mythology.

111

Again, whether or not Hazlitt's reference to the indissoluble ties that bind the heart to nature, to the secure repose—"elbow room and breathing space"—her beauties pledge, to the shady tree and brook, for illustration of these, to the lovely tales of Greek mythology which they engender—whether or not he looked toward Keats as he said these words and noted a smile of pleased recognition on the face of the young author of *Endymion* we cannot say. We can say that Keats understood this language and had expressed these thoughts at the opening of his poem. They appear more beautifully succinct in a passing observation in Book IV:

> The spirit culls
> Unfaded amaranth, when wild it strays
> Through the old garden-ground of boyish days.

And once again, proved with the testimony of bitter pulse, in the letter written under the gaze of death to James Rice,

> How astonishingly does the chance of leaving the world impress a sense of its natural beauties on us. Like poor Falstaff, though I do not babble, I think of green fields. I muse with the greatest affection on every flower I have known from my infancy—their shapes and coulours are as new to me as if I had just created them with a super-human fancy. It is because they are connected with the most thoughtless and happiest moments of our Lives (465).

THE POPPY CORONET

Once more to the opening passage: In the lines following those at which we broke off we find a comment upon the effect of beauty important not only in its psychological implication, but containing, I believe, a clue to the organics of the whole poem—

> but still will keep
> A bower quiet for us, and a sleep
> Full of sweet dreams, and health, and quiet breathing.

How taken Keats was with the mystery of sleep! He invoked the presence in a hymn so soothing that it might prevail to embalm the Soft Embalmer's self. He loitered in the regions of drowse and slow oblivion with a rich and still delight:

> Soft closer of our eyes!
> Low murmurer of tender lullabies!

Or, at times with half-humorous uneasiness:

> Dear Reynolds, as last night I lay in bed,
> There came before my eyes that wonted thread
> Of Shapes, and Shadows and Remembrances,
> That every other minute vex and please:
> Things all disjointed come from North and south,
> Two witch's eyes above a Cherub's mouth,
> Voltaire with casque and shield and Habergeon,
> And Alexander with his night-cap on—
> Old Socrates a tying his cravat;
> And Hazlitt playing with Miss Edgeworth's cat;
> And Junius Brutus pretty well so, so,

Making the best of's way towards Soho.
   Few are there who escape these visitings—
P'erhaps one or two, whose lives have patent wings;
And through whose curtains peeps no hellish nose,
No wild boar tushes, and no Mermaid's toes.

Certainly for this kind of mental experience on the margins of
sleep, Keats needed no book source. Yet he could read, in the
forty-fifth chapter of his copy of Locke's *Conduct,* a passage
wherein precisely this kind of experience is examined for psychological purposes:

> I have known in a case something of kin to this, though
> much odder, and that is of a sort of visions that some
> people have lying quiet but perfectly awake in the dark,
> or with their eyes shut. It is a great variety of faces, most
> commonly very odd ones, that appear to them in a train
> one after another; so that having had just the sight of the
> one, it immediately passes away to give place to another
> that the same instant succeeds and has as quick an exit
> as its leader, and so they march on in a constant succes-
> sion; nor can any one of them by any endeavour be
> stopped or retained beyond the instant of its appearance,
> but is thrust out by its follower, which will have its turn.
> Concerning this fantastical phenomenon I have talked
> with several people, whereof some have been perfectly
> acquainted with it, and others have been so wholly
> strangers to it, that they could hardly be brought to con-
> ceive or believe it.

There can be no doubt that Keats observed the work of the
mind in slumber with the keen curiosities both of poet and
psychologist. He knew that sleep and poetry are boon com-

rades, that Psyche keeps busy at her loom even while waking consciousness lies prone, and that her weaving is often purposive for the creation or the deeper comprehension of beauty. He speaks of the delightful and exciting conversations enjoyed in Haydon's studio as "making us wings" (for the night?) and on the impulse of such wings wrote "Sleep and Poetry," with express acknowledgment of his debt to sleep. The way in which the impact of beautiful objects or ideas is sustained and emphasized by the mind in slumber appears and reappears for comment in his speculations:

> Let him on a certain day read a certain Page of full Poesy or distilled Prose, and let him wander with it, and muse upon it, and reflect upon it, and bring home to it, and prophesy upon it, and dream upon it, until it becomes stale—but when will it do so? Never. When Man has arrived at a certain ripeness in intellect any one grand and spiritual passage serves him as a starting-post towards all "the two-and-thirty Palaces." How happy is such a voyage of conception, what delicious diligent Indolence! A doze upon a sofa does not hinder it, and a nap upon Clover engenders ethereal finger-pointings (103).

In "I stood tip-toe" he luxuriates in the evening primroses

> O'er which the mind may hover till it dozes;
> O'er which it well might take a pleasant sleep.

Let us again, by the hearsed and canonized bones of all source hunters, reject any notion that these speculations were merely literary. Keats writes ever of experience, but this was experience ratified and pointed by the thoughts and theories of the Associationist School. Beginning with Hobbes, the vivid working of the sense-engendered imagination in dreams is commonly noticed:

> As standing water, put into motion by the stroke of a stone or blast of wind doth not presently give over moving as soon as the wind ceaseth, or the stone settleth: so neither doth the effect close which the object hath wrought upon the brain, so soon as ever by turning aside of the organs, the object ceaseth to work; that is to say, though the sense be past, the image or conception remaineth; but more obscurely while we are awake . . . and this obscure conception is that we call phantasy or imagination . . . but where present sense is not, as in sleep, there the images remaining after sense when there be any as in dreams, are not obscure but strong and clear. . . . For sleep is the privation of the act of sense, (the power remaining) and dreams are the imaginations of them that sleep.—*The Elements of Law,* III

Hartley remarks that "dreams are nothing but the imaginations of a sleeping man," that "the trains of visible ideas which occur in dreams are far more vivid than common visible ideas." Dugald Stewart makes the point that we exercise no voluntary control over our ideas in dreams, but that they are very lively and follow customary pursuits; and Darwin in *The Loves of the Plants* asserts that "in sleep the organs of sense are closed or inert, and hence the trains of ideas associated in our imaginations are never interrupted or dissevered by the irritations of external objects. . . ." There was, of course, the convention, hallowed by Chaucer (as Keats thought) in "The Flower and the Leaf," of the formal dream vision. The concept of poet as dreamer is age-old. Psychological theory gave new meaning to these traditions, and, more important, it explained and confirmed Keats' own conviction of the mind's fertility in slumber. If trances in Nature, profound and sometimes painful reveries, musings in the shadowy margins of drowse had proved fecund, why not take the further license vouchsafed by psychology and explore the kindred and still more vivid action of the mind in dream? Why not enjoy in poetry the scope, and liberty, and spontaneous mental movement of dreaming, not as external artifice but as a discovered organic of the imagination?

In the middle of Book I of *Endymion* there occurs one of the finest of all Keats' sleep passages. Peona has brought her care-ridden brother to her own favorite bower on a river island and lulled him to rest on a couch of dried flower leaves. There follows this invocation:

> O magic sleep! O comfortable bird
> That broodest o'er the troubled sea of the mind
> Till it is hush'd and smooth! O unconfin'd
> Restraint! imprisoned liberty! great key
> To golden palaces, strange minstrelsy,
> Fountains grotesque, new trees, bespangled caves,
> Echoing grottos, full of tumbling waves
> And moonlight; aye, to all the mazy world
> Of silvery enchantment!

Amy Lowell's remarks on this passage are so penetrating and pertinent that they must be quoted in full:

> I think that few people have noticed the excellent psychology of this invocation. The comparative reason-

ableness of the "golden palaces" gives way to a music already somewhat "strange," which ushers in fountains with a touch of the grotesque about them. The trees are unlike those of the waking world, "bespangled caves" gives points of glittering light playing over darkness, the music sounds mellow and far, it repeats itself and echoes, ceases to be music, becoming instead the continued roar of waves, while the sparkling scintillations change to a broad and serene light, the sleeper is in a "mazy world" where contours merge and fade and all that remains is a silver efflorescence flooding a dazed feeling of delight. Then comes forgetfulness. Keats must have experienced just this sort of falling asleep a thousand times, as we all have if we stop to think of it.

This is admirable and renovating criticism. But it stops short of an observation most important, and clearly indicated at this point, namely, that in this passage are sketched the contours of the very silver and spell-fast world in which Endymion is to move. The passage is a catalogue, almost, of the regions and atmospheres to be developed in the course of the poem. Palaces, minstrelsy, spangled caves, echoing grottoes, and moonlight are, by the poet's statement, characteristic fabrications of the mind in slumber, and of these structures not one fails to emerge on Endymion's path with marvelous elaboration.

And sleep itself as an event and as a symbol appears repeatedly in the poem. We shall speak presently of how the elements of *Endymion* blend and blur to strange composites, and of the accidents and chances whereby the plot is developed. The story, such as there is, is punctuated by recurrent climaxes, wherein Endymion attains to the presence of his heavenly love. These moments are described in terms of flight toward heaven, flight in imagination, flight into dream, so closely intermingled as to prove the virtual identity in Keats' mind of all three. We have noticed the flight in sleep in Book IV, and the explicit identification of this flight as of the imagination. Attainment in that passage was preluded by sleep. So is it regularly in the poem. The first, enamoring vision of Book I shows how close, in Keats' mind, was the association of sleep and imagination. Endymion, refreshed by the sleep to which Peona had lulled him, tells of the origin of his cares; how one day he came suddenly upon a magic bed of ditamy and poppies:

> And, sitting down close by, began to muse
> What it might mean. . . .
>
> .   .   .   .   .   .
>
>   Thus on I thought,
> Until my head was dizzy and distraught.
> Moreover, through the dancing poppies stole
> A breeze, most softly lulling to my soul;
> And shaping visions all about my sight
>
> .   .   .   .   .   .
>
> And then I fell asleep.
> Ah, can I tell
> The enchantment that afterwards befel?
> Yet it was but a dream: yet such a dream . . .

He dreams that the doors of heaven open for his flight. Fearful to alight from such high soaring, he spreads imaginary pinions wide and presently sees emerging from the clouds "the loveliest moon, that ever silver'd o'er a shell" for Neptune. The moon is presently veiled in clouds, and there appears a "bright something," "completed form of all completeness," a golden-haired lady in a blue scarf. At the touch of her hand he faints, yet holds his recollection, and in a dreamy swoon is lapped and lulled by her along the dangerous sky. Soon the lovers are wafted down to a flowery Alp. Here is "store of newest joys," but here again sleep overtakes him— a dream of sleep, within a dream of sleep, within a dream!

In the second book there is another apex of attainment, reached by way of dreaming. An eagle has brought Endymion to a jasmine bower. He feels every sense "grown ethereal for pleasure," and prays to his unknown love that she will at least let him come to her in dream:

> Thus spake he, and that moment felt endued
> With power to dream deliciously.

Casting himself upon a mossy bed, he stretched forth his arms into the air "and took, O bliss! a naked waist." There follows an ardent passage of fondling and endearments, after which he wakes to loneliness once more.

Yet another dreamy swoon marks the climax of Book III, where at the height of the revelry in Neptune's hall,

> The palace whirls
> Around giddy Endymion; seeing he
> Was there far strayed from mortality.
> He could not bear it—shut his eyes in vain;
> Imagination gave a dizzier pain.
> 'O I shall die! sweet Venus, be my stay!
> Where is my lovely mistress? Well-away!

I die— I hear her voice— I feel my wing— '
At Neptune's feet he sank. . . .

.   .   .   .   .   .

To his inward senses these words spake aloud;
Written in star-light on the dark above:
Dearest Endymion!

All of these passages indicate that in *Endymion* Keats sym-
bolizes the action of the imagination by sleep. And yet the
relation of the two in his mind is closer and more organic
than that of symbol to fact. In these dreamy flights neither
the hero nor the reader is quite sure whether the event is a
dream of sleep or a daydream of fancy. In Book II, for example, there is a flight toward his goddess which, although it
is described in language exactly similar to that in which the
dream flights are described, proves in the end to be a voyage of
waking fancy. Holding his head to keep off "the burr of
smothering fancies," started there by a suddenly appearing
naiad, Endymion sits down to muse upon

the war, the deeds,
The disappointment, the anxiety,
Imagination's struggles, far and nigh.

He prays to the moon to temper his love, and then to tie large
wings upon his shoulders. Even as he prays, he feels that he is
soaring toward her:

'By all the stars
That tend thy bidding, I do think the bars
That kept my spirit in are burst—that I
Am sailing with thee through the dizzy sky!

How beautiful thou art! The world how deep!
How tremulous-dazzlingly the wheels sweep
Around their axle! Then these gleaming reins,
How lithe! When this thy chariot attains
Its airy goal, haply some bower veils
Those twilight eyes? Those eyes!—my spirit fails—
Dear goddess, help! or the wide-gaping air
Will gulph me—help!'—At this with madden'd stare,
And lifted hands, and trembling lips he stood;
Like old Deucalion mountain'd o'er the flood.

One might venture to say that in this passage the symbolic
relationship is reversed; that the flight of fancy here symbol-
izes sleep and dreaming. But the fact is that in this kind of
fluctuant and simultaneous symbolizing, identifying, and dis-
criminating of elements, Keats is not merely suggesting—he is
in fact exemplifying—the close kinship between imagination
and the sleep work of the mind, presenting in poetry not only
the luminous atmospheres and apparitions of slumber but the
multiplied and equivocal texture of dream thought.

Well known among the liberties of the dreaming mind is
the trick of combining diverse elements of experience and
representing them within the frame of a single and apparently
homogeneous event, still vaguely felt to consist of disparate
parts. Hartley observed how "the same person appears in two
places at the same time; two persons appearing successively in
the same place coalesce into one." We dream that father is
himself, and still not himself, but the invalid around the cor-
ner. This is called composition and everywhere recognized as
typical of dream work. It is commonly agreed, also, that the
dreamer's self is often a discernible part in these composite

structures, his proper ego or an aspect of his nature projected upon a figure of the dream.

Now the repeated and surprising emergence of John Keats and his personal problems and preoccupations in the person and problems of Endymion is a fact of common remark by critics of the poem. Sir Sidney Colvin writes:

> Keats works in part from his own mental experience. He weaves into his tale, in terms always of concrete imagery, all the complex fluctuations of joy and despondency, gleams of confident spiritual illumination, alternating with faltering hours of darkness and self doubt, which he had been himself undergoing since the ambition to be a great poet seized him.

Similarly Amy Lowell:

> Endymion's love for Diana is both Keats' story, merely as story, and Keats' own life and work, especially his work on this poem.

She considers the injunction put upon Endymion by the fountain nymph—

> 'Thou must wander far
> In other regions, past the scanty bar
> To mortal steps, before thou cans't be ta'en
> From every wasting sigh, from every pain,
> Into the gentle bosom of thy love'—

as composed in part of Keats' own warning to himself that he must grow and change to be worthy of his own conception, and must endure through struggle to the achievement of his poem.

The difference between *Endymion* and proper allegory turns, in fact, on this point. It is the difference between "an extended metaphor" in which relations are consistent and elements distinct, and the intermittent, composite, and ever personal symbolizing of the dream. In Keats' poem, the Carian shepherd-prince speaks rather inappropriately of

Imagination's struggles, far and nigh.

Keats describes Endymion's sensations and perplexities in terms elsewhere used to describe very personal ones of his own. When Endymion cries out,

'I
Have no self passion, or identity,'

he is using the words Keats used to describe his own curious sense of self-annulment in the presence of difficult or embarrassing circumstances:

His [Tom's] identity presses upon me so all day that I am obliged to go out—(216).

A Poet is the most unpoetical of any thing in existence; because he has no Identity. . . .When I am in a room with People if I ever am free from speculating on creations of my own brain, then not myself goes home to myself: but the identity of every one in the room begins to to [*sic*] press upon me that I am in a very little time an[ni]hilated (228).

Endymion's depression, when he sits wearily "before the maw Of a wide outlet"

> And thoughts of self came on, how crude and sore
> The journey homeward to habitual self!

is Keats' depression after a flight of the mind, such as that prefigured by the charioteer in "Sleep and Poetry":

> The visions all are fled—the car is fled
> Into the light of heaven, and in their stead
> A sense of real things comes doubly strong,
> And, like a muddy stream, would bear along
> My soul to nothingness.

In the famous "Cave of Quietude" in Book IV Keats is ascribing to Endymion one of his own moods of depression, of which the letters speak so movingly. These obvious self-identifications are not systematic and purposive in the manner of allegory, but appear in the involuntary, abrupt, and irrational composition of the dream. Of a poem so composed, it is surely vain to demand a systematic allegory. Rather to be expected are arbitrary and impulsive movements of thought and image, chance-determined developments of plot, trivial modes of relation, and clusters rather than sequences of meaning.

"In the dream," says Volkelt (quoted by Freud), "the ideas chase and hunt each other on the strength of accidental similarities and barely perceptible connections. All dreams are pervaded by such loose and free associations."

The reviewers, Croker and Jeffrey, complain of precisely this quality in Endymion:

> He wanders from one subject to another, from the association, not of ideas, but of sounds, and the work is composed of hemistichs which it is quite evident have

forced themselves upon the author by the mere force of
the catchwords on which they turn.——CROKER

It seems as if the author had ventured everything that occurred to him in the shape of a glittering image, or
striking expression—taken the first word that presented
itself to make up a rhyme, and then made that word the
germ of a new cluster of images—and so wandered on,
equally forgetful whence he came and heedless whither
he was going.——JEFFREY

This is no more than the truth. In many parts of the poem the
thought runs in random pursuit of echo, usually the echo of
rhyme. For example, in the first book, where Keats describes
the forest on Latmos:

> Upon the sides of Latmos was outspread
> A mighty forest.

This is the most direct way possible into the subject, but one
may guess by what follows that this simplicity is the simplicity of the first-occurring idea rather than the painfully
achieved simplicity of art. It gets Keats into immediate trouble, at any rate, for the next two and one-half lines snarl themselves around the hooks of rhyme:

> For the moist earth fed
> So plenteously all weed-hidden roots
> Into o'er-hanging boughs, and precious fruits.

It takes no Croker to see that *fed* comes only to rescue *spread*,
that it lugs after it the ideas of *earth* and *roots,* which are in
turn barely saved by *fruits.* Having come to a period, Keats

starts again, with what seems again to be the first-offering idea:

> And it had gloomy shades, sequestered deep,
> Where no man went.

Deep seduces him to the strained phrase, "if from shepherd's keep," which is followed by an account of a local superstition so incompletely and perplexingly uttered that we may suppose it to derive from no profounder mythopeic source than the exigency of rhyme:

> And if from shepherd's keep
> A lamb strayed far a-down those inmost glens,
> Never again saw he the happy pens
> Whither his brethren, bleating with content,
> Over the hills at every nightfall went.
> Among the shepherds, 'twas believed ever,
> That not one fleecy lamb which thus did sever
> From the white flock, but pass'd unworried
> By angry wolf, or pard with prying head,
> Until it came to some unfooted plains
> Where fed the herds of Pan: ay great his gains
> Who thus one lamb did lose.

The plot, I suspect, evolves likewise by accident, although not precisely the accident of rhyme. There is in fact, no plot at all in the first two books, merely a series of episodes, the hero moved from one event to another by being made to swoon and wake up somewhere else. In Book III, we are given a story, the story of Glaucus: how he loved Scylla, was beguiled into forsaking her by Circe, "arbitrary queen of sense," and as a penalty for attempting to flee from this enchantress, condemned to a thousand years of old age under the sea. At Glaucus' bidding, Endymion performs certain rites, and so doing, restores youth to Glaucus and life to Scylla and a multitude of drowned lovers. This is a plot, though it is Glaucus' plot.

But in Book IV Endymion suddenly acquires a plot of his own. He falls in love with an Indian Maid and is torn with a sense of divided allegiance to her and to the lady of his dreams, until, in the end, he finds that the two are one. Many people regard this conflict of affections as highly allegorical. The Indian Maid is said to represent "the dark side of the moon," or "the newer phases on which the imagination has entered," or "sensuous passion," or "nature," or "humanity in trouble," according to the inclination of the allegorist. Finney, moreover, finds for her a literary ancestry—that Keats took the divided love theme from Drayton's "Endymion and Phoebe." Certainly the duality of being, shared by Cynthia and the Maid, tempts to symbolical interpretation. The Indian Maid could easily represent the sense-bred imagination, the Corybantian trance seizure, the faculty second lowest in the association scale, hence not quite respectable, and Cynthia the loftier truth-attaining faculty of imagination, dear to Wordsworth. The identification of these two as one faculty would confirm and illustrate that rearrangement of the Hartleian scale we suspected in the "pleasure-thermometer." But this symbolic relationship, if in fact it existed in Keats' mind, could hardly be taken as the meaning planned for the whole poem. It seems unlikely that Keats would have deliberately waited till the last book to bring the mysterious lady from behind a bush and give her the plot.

There is possibly a simpler explanation of this theme, one that better accords with the impulsive and unpremeditated fashion of the whole. Near the beginning of Book III there is an impassioned tribute by Endymion to moonlight, but sung at least partly in Keats' own voice:

'What is there in thee, Moon! that thou shouldst move
My heart so potently? When yet a child
I oft have dried my tears when thou hast smil'd.
Thou seem'dst my sister: hand in hand we went
From eve to morn across the firmament.
No apples would I gather from the tree,
Till thou hadst cool'd their cheeks deliciously:
No tumbling water ever spake romance,
But when my eyes with thine thereon could dance:
No woods were green enough, no bower divine,
Until thou liftedst up thine eyelids fine:
In sowing time ne'er would I dibble take,
Or drop a seed, till thou wast wide awake;
And, in the summer tide of blossoming,
No one but thee hath heard me blithely sing
And mesh my dewy flowers all the night.
No melody was like a passing spright
If it went not to solemnize thy reign.
Yes, in my boyhood, every joy and pain
By thee were fashion'd to the self-same end;
And as I grew in years, still didst thou blend
With all my ardours: thou wast the deep glen;
Thou wast the mountain-top—the sage's pen—
The poet's harp—the voice of friends—the sun;
Thou wast the river—thou wast glory won;
Thou wast my clarion's blast—thou wast my steed—
My goblet full of wine—my topmost deed:—,
Thou wast the charm of women, lovely Moon!'

In the two thousand preceding lines of *Endymion* we have
heard nothing at all of this hero's lifelong cult of moonlight.
But Keats was taking nightly walks with Bailey along the
streams of Oxford, and critics agree that the poet's own feelings beautifully shape these lines. However, by allowing Endymion to say them, Keats has suddenly endowed him with an
object of worship other than the dream-lady, the obsessing
mistress, he has all along been seeking. The theme of dual
love has emerged by accident.

Now abruptly Glaucus is introduced. Amy Lowell believes
that he got into the story merely because Keats happened to
be living at the time in the classical atmosphere of Bailey's
Oxford room, with Ovid on the shelves. In Ovid's story of
Glaucus, there is no succumbing to Circe, no clash of loyalties.
Circe, however, is referred to as passion and voluptuous sense,
and Scylla as a "faire intelligence." Since conflict in loves has
suggested itself by chance, Keats allows it to shape Glaucus'
tale, and accordingly develops and stresses the hinted contrast
in the natures of the two ladies. By this time, he has brought
Glaucus and Endymion into a somewhat parallel case. What
more natural than to stress the parallel, endow Endymion with
a beguiling and dangerous mistress, give her a little of Circe's
sensuality, and since the fact of double identity was latent in
the first haphazard emergence of the moon-mistress conflict,
knit up the tale on his hook, and let the loose ends (and they
are many) flutter brightly in the wind?

Of such strange and baffling "compositions and decompositions of the intellect"—chance echoes of rhyme shaping the
thought, figures and apparitions composed in part from impressions of the evening's walk, in part from the book lately

thumbed through, and in part from tensions more profound and habitual—is *Endymion* made. And the plot is mere impromptu variation on a theme brought to mind by chance. The poem is a product almost pure of that use of the mind which association called imaginative, "knowing no stop in its delight, but going where it listeth." In dream, as psychology assured him, the faculty worked most vividly; "the check of the senses being removed, the trains of ideas are not interrupted or dissevered." Keats tried this theory in *Endymion,* and the trial was not wholly successful. But the poem is not to be dismissed as a mere inept and bungled tale, nor yet explained as a planned allegory. The incoherence of a broken dream is no accident. Sleep is the leitmotif. The complex allegory shifts and recenters with each new apparition, and perhaps contains deep secrets of the poet's nature, beyond our ken. It is the fluctuant allegory of the dream.

"*They had in common with the greatest, a quality of sensuous thought, or of thinking with the senses, or of the senses thinking, of which the exact formula remains to be described.*"

—T. S. ELIOT

CHAPTER FOUR

THE SIMPLE
IMAGINATIVE MIND

JOHN KEATS professed poetry
with all his heart. He wanted at all costs to write it nobly, to
be among the English poets at his death. He dedicated himself
to this clear vocation surely not later than that April morning
in 1817 when he wrote from Mrs. Cooke's lodginghouse on
the Isle of Wight:

> I find that I cannot exist without poetry—without
> eternal poetry—half the day will not do—the whole of
> it— I began with a little, but habit has made me a Levia-
> than— I had become all in a Tremble from not having
> written any thing of late—the Sonnet over leaf did me
> some good. I slept the better last night for it (21).

This passionate commitment to his art is not merely important in the story of Keats' mind. It is the pregnant and initial
circumstance from which that story rises and unfolds. For it
implies a commitment equally unreserved to the authority of
the imagination, its lights, its pleasures, and its pains. The
story of Keats' efforts to validate the imagination, to prove its
compass, and to reconcile its pains is the essential story of his
creative life.

This problem of the imagination was at once clarified and complicated by the new psychology. The theory of association presented it as a definite and describable faculty, explaining its mechanics and affirming it as an integral part of normal mentality. In this light it could no longer be regarded as a mystery, nor a mood, nor a hazy, wayward humor of thought, nor a mantle to be assumed and doffed by the poetic soul upon appropriate occasions. On the other hand, it presented the life-in-imagination as a mere stage in mental growth, an early one in which the properly developing mind did not long tarry. Keats, like any other poet, knew that, whatever its ultimate nature, the imagination was the faculty by which he lived, the gift that marked him as a poet. To the stern relegation of this gift as lowest but one in the scale of mental experience he could not possibly subscribe. Nor could the other poets of his time. Wordsworth evaded the sentence by a radical revision of Hartley, investing the imagination with a mantle of sanctity and ascribing to it high contemplative powers. Coleridge, "completely overthrowing Hartley, and all modern infidels," made it the instrument of true knowledge, the shaping virtue that men share with God.

To the untheological and untheoretical Keats these ways of solving the dilemma were evidently not satisfactory. To be sure, he tried them from time to time. When he wrote to Bailey that the imagination is "a Shadow of reality to come— . . . that we shall enjoy ourselves here after by having what we call happiness on Earth repeated in a finer tone . . . ," he approached the theologizing vein. But this was not a considered and permanent conclusion. It was, as the context makes clear, a "speculation." And Keats indulged at times in other and contradictory speculations. There are in his comments on the imagination traces, indeed, of many trial attitudes, and they indicate perhaps chiefly that he was not primarily concerned with generalizations, with fitting the concept of the imagination into a structure of other concepts.

What concerned him, in fact, was the place of the imagination, not *sub specie aeternitatis,* but in the daily activity of his own mind. His pulses told him that it was "a faculty closely allied to sense," that it was wild and irrational in its action, that it was the mark and charge of the poet, and that he, being a poet, must integrate its energies in his whole manner of being and thinking. Neither apotheosis nor half-faced fellowship would do. And so, for all of his wavering and contradictory theorizing about the imagination, we can see in the actual method of Keats' writing a steady tendency to preserve its wild, sensuous qualities and to extend its uses, to live by this talent which made him a poet, in and out of hours, and (paradoxically) to reach such conclusions as he could regarding the place and value of the faculty by use of the faculty itself.

His effort to live by the imagination was a painful effort. It involved him in distress of nerves, in distress of conscience (of a peculiar kind), and it involved him in some rather startling experiments in the conventions of thought and language. As for his nerves, the bardic trance, the unreproved coursings of the mind, brought at times visions of fair places, feelings of mastery, joy-freighted moments "when those who love the bay, fly from all sorrowing"; but joy was not always the seamark of this sailing. There were, as we have seen, dark harbors as well, and in the fidelity of his report of experience, Keats

JOHN KEATS' FANCY

does not omit notice of these. "Sickly imagination" casts its
wan light over the sonnet written at Burns' tomb. Terror and
dismay lurk, as we have seen, in other labyrinths of dream.
After describing, in the "Epistle to Reynolds," the grotesque
train of drowsy images, Keats cries out in something like despair:

> O that our dreamings all of sleep or wake
> Would all their colours from the Sunset take:
> From something of material sublime,
> Rather than shadow our own Soul's daytime
> In the dark void of Night.

Here is an unvarnished report of the poet's one talent, quite
the opposite in spirit from Wordsworthian apotheosis. It was,
of course, inevitable that Keats' profound plumbings of consciousness should bring with them tumult, instability of
mood, elations and depressions, and at times seem to carry
away, in their whirlwind violence, the poet's "self-passion and
identity." It was hard to know what to make of these storms.
Sometimes they seemed the very ratification of his poet's
nature:

> As to the poetical Character itself (I mean that sort of
> which, if I am any thing, I am a Member; that sort dis-
> tinguished from the wordsworthian or egotistical sub-
> lime; which is a thing per se and stands alone) it is not
> itself—it has no self—it is every thing and nothing—
> It has no character—it enjoys light and shade; it lives
> in gusto, be it foul or fair, high or low, rich or poor,
> mean or elevated— It has as much delight in conceiving
> an Iago as an Imogen. . . . A Poet is the most unpo-
> etical of any thing in existence; because he has no
> Identity (227-228).

But life in gusto was exhausting; and he yearned at times for a quieter one, "to compose without this fever," to "substitute a more thoughtful and quiet power." There are those who would see in Keats' recurrent wish for calm the dominant theme of his life. Yet, as late as August, 1819, he is writing to Reynolds that it would be vain to endeavor after a more reasonable way of writing.

> If you should have any reason to regret this state of excitement in me, I will turn the tide of your feelings in the right Channel, by mentioning that it is the only state for the best sort of Poetry—that is all I care for, all I live for (374).

The problem here is mainly one of the sheer physical and mental stress which the life-in-imagination involved.

There was also the ethical problem. Keats knew that the world which the imagination pioneers is, in a certain sense, pivoted in self. Whirling on its own axis, the mind moves in limitless arcs; it can form

> greater things—that is to say ethereal things———but here I am talking like a Madman greater things that [for than] our Creator himself made (31)!!

Not like a madman quite, but certainly more like a sentimental belletrist than a firm-handed worker in the art. Here is again a touch of the romantic awe toward the imagination more characteristic of others of his time than of Keats. For although he advised Shelley to curb his magnanimity—that an artist "must have 'self-concentration'—selfishness, perhaps," Keats was not temperamentally self-centered, and he knew life could not be forever lived in a poet's dream. Beyond the concentric and opulent world of trance lay another world of pains and troubles which he at no time of his life forgot. Again, this perplexing sense of disparate realms of fact and fancy has been made the theme of Keats' life, and we are told that Keats' growing up was merely a slow process of deciding to face fact. But it has been rightly observed that the claims of "real life" assert themselves in his very early work. In the 1815 "Epistle to Mathew" he proposes to put on "soft humanity" and tell of those who have fallen in the cause of freedom; and in "Sleep and Poetry" the daydream of nymphs and leafy worlds is broken off with admonitions of "a nobler life," full of the agonies of human hearts.

The emotional throes and the ethical problems of the life-in-imagination are referred to again and again in Keats' poetry and letters. Their shadows drift across *Endymion* and they are the subjects of the two "Hyperion" poems. In the earlier of these, as I have elsewhere tried to show, the calm and bovine Titans fall before the passionate god of poetry. In the second the intention seems to be to reverse the thesis and present the feverish poet as a weak dreamer, "Bearing more woe than all his sins deserve." But this attempt ends in a snarl of fine distinctions between dreamers, poets, servants of humanity, and humanistic poets, eloquent in its very confusion. All this has been much rehearsed in books about Keats.

Less commonly remarked, perhaps because less dramatic, is the problem which he had to face (in his fidelity to the imagination) of practically integrating the sense-engendered faculty with other faculties of the mind for the everyday development and communication of ideas—in his letters, that is, and in ordinary discourse. The conventions here seemed to exclude the spontaneous swarmings of ideas, to distort the electric actuality of the mind's life, to require that a poet turn off his imagination between whiles and think like a "consequitive man." To the whole-souled and dedicated poet Keats, no such arbitrary intermission was possible. The virtues of the imagination could not be confined within the conventions of verse. And with extraordinary boldness and still more extraordinary insight into the dynamics of thinking he directed the imagination, the train of associations closely allied to sense, beyond the borders of poetry and into regions new and strange. We see its wild and magic power working in his letters.

THE LOADSTONE
CONCATENATION

Keats wrote extraordinarily fine letters. There is a sense in which the book of them might be called better than the book of his poems, though it would be surely a sense fraught with exceptions. At any rate, no one would deny them the right to be called superlative examples of a nearly lost art—great things of their kind. I do not speak now of the letters to his sweetheart; they are a special matter, recording tensions more acute and biological than abide our question. They have produced in their time powerful disturbance in the minds of Matthew Arnold and some others, whom Keats had not in view in writing them. The beautiful and graceful and elegant and strange Miss Brawne, whom he had in view, was perhaps better pleased. With which remark, we put them by.

The gaiety, pathos, tenderness, speed, variety, strength of the others dazzle the mind. And the tone of each is so delicately tempered to the receptivity of each present correspondent that one could almost reconstruct the personalities of Keats' friends from his ways of writing to them. "I wish," he remarks in one, "I knew always the humour my friends would be in at opening a letter of mine, to suit it to them [as] nearly as possible. I could always find an egg shell for Melancholy and as for Merriment a Witty humour will turn any thing to Account." He knew, at any rate, and matched their usual tempers. Has he to address the megalomaniacal Haydon, mock-heroic painter of bad heroic pictures, who passed his days solemnly in debt and delusion of grandeur, Keats' own language grows orotund, his mental gestures sweeping. He opens with lines from *Love's Labour's Lost:*

> Let Fame, which all hunt after in their Lives,
> Live register'd upon our brazen tombs. . . .

> To think that I have no right to couple myself with you in this speech would be death to me so I have e'en written it—and I pray God that our brazen Tombs be nigh neighbors. . . . It is as well if you have not been teased with that Money affair—that bill-pestilence (29).

To touch the fourteen-year-old mind of his sister, his lines assume the very gravity, tender decorum, and shy merriment of the adolescent girl:

My dear Fanny,
    Let us now begin a regular question and answer—a

little pro and con; letting it interfere as a pleasant method of my coming at your favorite little wants and enjoyments, that I may meet them in a way befitting a brother (37).

There is a Leigh Huntian archness of fancy in his letter to Hunt, signed with the so-Huntian alias Junkets:

> My dear Hunt,
>   The little Gentleman that sometimes lurks in a gossips bowl ought to have come in very likeness of a *coasted* [*sic*] crab and choked me outright for not having answered your Letter (22).

A matter-of-fact vigor in those to the dynamic Brown, a tone of serious regard to the eternal aspects in the cleric, Bailey's, and a delicious inconsequence of poet's double-talk in those to Reynolds, another "Muse's son of promise." All this, of course, is evidence of the "camelion" nature which he ascribed to the poet and confessed to in himself; his epistolary hand inevitably takes a shade of color from each of his correspondents—an excellent thing in a letter writer.

Quick sympathies and delicate flexibility are remarkable in these letters. But there is another quality, more pervasive and perhaps rarer in the degree in which Keats realizes it, namely, their rich texture. His simplest communications come off with a full-blooded, full-bodied utterance, with an appeal to a wide range of responses, that imply and invite awareness of a great number of things. This plenitude and savor are what we should expect in a poet, but in Keats' letters, they illustrate a temper and habit—indeed a dynamic—of thinking which is, in a literal sense, imaginative.

He has, let us say, to confirm an appointment with his good mentor, Charles Cowden Clarke, to get a bit of information about time and place, and to throw out, by the way, an invitation to call when convenient. He does it this way:

My daintie Davie,
  I will be as punctual as the Bee to the Clover. Very glad am I at the thoughts of seeing so soon this glorious Haydon and all his creation. I pray thee let me know when you go to Ollier's and where he resides—this I forgot to ask you—and tell me also when you will help me waste a sullen day— God 'ield you—

J K (8-9).

The bark of communicative purpose glides straight across its brief course to harbor, and its freight of actual meaning is liker to the tin trays of practical life than to

Manna and dates, in argosy transferr'd.

But with it moves a small flight of images, recollections, impulses, attitudes, gracing the voyage like a cloud of gulls. Upon the staid and immediate identity of Clarke is imposed the covenanting minister Davie—

Leeze me on thy curly pow, Daintie Davie—

his gentle, generous protectress, and Burns, Scotland, and song. With the figure of the five-foot Cockney poet, hand on knocker, merges the golden bee, shooting like a bullet to the summer-sunny meadow. The nebula of poetry—verse at least—hovers around the inversion, "very glad am I," ("What a bright boy am I," etc.). "This glorious Haydon" looms refulgent, looking upon his own works and calling them good. The character of a specifically imaged day is carried in "sullen," with further hints of lowering faces and the mutter of tongues, or thunder. And with the final "God 'ield you," he involves perhaps Ophelia, and her painful garland and shattering world. The blank matter of meeting on time provides the portals to a dozen infinities. A simple situation has been enriched from the store of Keats' sensations—remembrance of things past. Enrichment of experience, we know, is the special way of poetry; in fact, the way of aesthetic contemplation of events. "In practical activity," as the aestheticians point out, "we reduce to the minimum the qualities of events, because the whole aim of the activity is to expunge a disrupting quality. . . . But quality is the heart of aesthetic experience, the more vivid and extensive the quality, the richer the experience." [7] There is rich quality, obviously, in Keats' note to Clarke. In this note the range of reference is wide in mental space—from Ollier's to Ophelia. But the same effect, though perhaps in less degree, is often brought about by the introduction of more proximate items, lists of synonymous, or of related attributes, a trick Keats doubtless admired in Rabelais, and, for that matter, in "blown Jack" Falstaff. "I am glad," he writes to Fanny Keats,

> you got on so well with Monsr. le Curè—is he a nice Clergyman—a great deal depends upon a cock'd hat and powder—not gun powder, lord love us, but lady-meal, violet-smooth, dainty-scented lilly-white, feather-soft, wigsby-dressing, coat-collar-spoiling whisker-reaching, pig-tail loving, swans down-puffing, parson-sweetening powder (294).

And, to the Reynolds sisters:

> There you are among sands, stones, Pebbles, Beeches, Cliffs, Rocks, Deeps, Shallows, weeds, ships Boats (at a distance) Carrots, Turnips, Sun, Moon, and Stars, and all those sort of things—here am I among Colleges, halls, Stalls, Plenty of Trees, thank God (35).

"Buy· a girdle—," he warns Reynolds,

> put a pebble in your Mouth—loosen your Braces—for I am going among Scenery whence I intend to tip you the Damosel Radcliffe— I'll cavern you, and grotto you, and waterfall you, and wood you, and water you, and immense-rock you, and tremendous-sound you, and solitude you (114).

Feux de joie around the batteries of Fort-St-Hyphen de-Phrase is the name Keats gave to these troopings of synonyms, and they serve in their way to enrich many a simple statement. The collocations in these are less startling than those in the Clarke note; the items lead to one another with a more obvious relevance. Yet, it is a difference only of degree, and for the reader who likes these Rabelaisian catalogues, this same sense of plenitude, of a number of things brought surprisingly to enrich what might have been the jejune circumstances— wig-powder, seascape, mountains—is active.

> More for delyt than world to multiplie,

says Chaucer in a quite other connection.

The "God 'ield you" at the close of the Clarke note is a bit of pedantry, with a transparent relevance. A formula of blessing is brought from Shakespeare to the conventional need for one at the end of a letter. In the letter to Reynolds just quoted there is collision more abrupt and surprising:

> I went to the Theatre here the other night which I forgot to tell George, and got insulted, which I ought to remember to forget to tell any Body; for I did not fight, and as yet have had no redress—"Lie thou there, sweetheart!" (114).

Into the parenthesis staggers the roistering Pistol:

> Fear we broadsides? No, let the fiend give fire:
> Give me some sack, and sweetheart, lie thou there.

The contretemps at the Teignmouth Theatre flashes up with the fire of Mistress Quickly's hearth at the Boar's Head Tavern. This juxtaposition is brought off without either verbal (as, like) or evident logical (related qualities of wig powder) connections. The sanction for Pistol lies in slightly more private regions of Keats' mind, and has a degree of that capriciousness which private relevancies seem to have. Such caprice is common in Keats' letters:

> Does Shelley go on telling strange Stories of the Death of Kings? Tell him there are strange Stories of the death of Poets—some have died before they were conceived "how do you make that out Master Vellum." Does M^rs. S. cut Bread and Butter as neatly as ever (26–27)?

> Perhaps I may have done a good deal [of poetry] for the time but it appears such a Pin's Point to me that I will not coppy any out. When I consider that so many of these Pin points go to form a Bodkin point (God send I end not my Life with a bare Bodkin, in its modern sense) and that it requires a thousand bodkins to make a Spear . . . (26).

145

"Why should Woman suffer?" Aye. Why should she? 'By heavens I'd coin my very Soul and drop my Blood for Drachmas"! These things are (84).

Reynolds, of course, saw in a moment how Pistol got there and a bodkin's point will direct any one to Hamlet, but the intermedia are, so to speak, moving inward, the points of connection tending to the more personal and less conventional. Great minds jump, and there is need.

Here is a still more arbitrary piece of joinery:

I believe you [knew] I went to Richards's—it was so whoreson a Night that I stopped there all the next day— His Remembrances to you. (Ext from the common place Book of my Mind— Mem— Wednesday— Hampstead—call in Warner Street—a Sketch of M^r. Hunt[)]—I will ever consider you my sincere and affectionate friend (12–13).

What ties bind these affairs together only Keats knows. This is a rather special kind of enrichment. What is most interesting is that he here gives a more or less local habitation and name ("the common place Book of my Mind") to that fluent, lawless, vivid welter of stored ideas whence all these valuable intrusions are drawn. This is, of course, the associative process, the imagination, or as we now call it, the stream of consciousness. William James' description of it is classic, and worth recalling; for it stresses the fact which Keats realized, with extraordinary psychological insight, of the constant activity and interplay of this stream in all kinds of thinking.

Every definite image in the mind is steeped and dyed in the free water that flows around it. With it goes the sense of its relations, near and remote, the dying echo whence it came to us, the dawning sense of whither it is to lead. The significance, the value of the image is all in this halo or penumbra that surrounds and escorts it.

All of us today are aware of this resourceful flood in ourselves, as the region of vital connections, of lightning play of appetites and aversions, and we probe its depth for the true dynamics of being. We have seen how John Keats allowed its luxurious drift to determine the direction of *Endymion,* how he prefigured it in the metaphor of flight, and how he poured its content into the early poems. But as a psychological, rather than a strictly artistic phenomenon, it engaged him also. The constant play of his "prose" mind, its bizarre and swift and at times seemingly irrational combinations fascinated him—his own and others.

> My head is sometimes in such a whirl in considering the million likings and antipathies of our Moments—that I can get into no settled strain in my Letters (176).

> Twelve days have pass'd since your last reached me—what has gone through the myriads of human Minds since the 12th we talk of the immense number of Books, the Volumes ranged thousands by thousands—but perhaps more goes through the human intelligence in 12 days than ever was written (83).

Hazlitt had, by the way, made a very similar observation in *Table Talk:* "How many ideas and trains of sentiment, long, deep and intense often pass through the mind in only one day's thinking or reading for instance."

The fine inconsequence of these compositions and decompositions of the intellect is naturally often a joking matter:

The whole [play] was made up of a virtuous young woman, an indignant brother, a suspecting lover, a libertine prince, a gratuitous villain, a street in Naples, a Cypress grove, lilies and roses, virtue and vice, a bloody sword, a spangled jacket, one Lady Olivia, one Miss O'Neil alias Evadne, alias Bellamira, alias—(Alias— Yea, and I say unto you a greater than Elias— There was Abbot, and talking of Abbot his name puts me in mind of a spelling book lesson, descriptive of the whole Dramatis personae—Abbot—Abbess—Actor—Actress—). The play is a fine amusement (311).

To Reynolds he wrote:

If I scribble long letters I must play my vagaries. I must be too heavy, or too light, for whole pages— I must be quaint and free of Tropes and figures— I must play my draughts as I please, and for my advantage and your erudition, crown a white with a black, or a black with a white, and move into black or white, far and near as I please— I must go from Hazlitt to Patmore, and make Wordsworth and Coleman play at leap-frog—or keep one of them down a whole half-holiday at fly the garter —"from Gray to Gay, from Little to Shakespeare" (142).

I should stop here quiet and comfortable in my theory of Nettles. You will see however I am obliged to run wild, being attracted by the Loadstone Concatenation (122–123).

This is excellent foppery, and on the face of it nothing else. Yet the loadstone concatenation prevailed to draw Keats from the surface of logical convention toward the center of private symbol and bizarre equivalent on occasions where such flight inward sorted oddly with the decorum of conversation.

I will tell you— Two most unfortunate and paral[l]el slips. . . . A friend says to me 'Keats I shall go and see Severn this Week' 'Ah' says I 'You want him to take your Portrait' and again 'Keats' says a friend 'When will you come to town again' 'I will' says I 'let you have the Mss next week' In both these I appear'd to attribute and [*for an*] interested motive to each of my friends' questions—the first made him flush; the second made him look angry— And yet I am innocent—in both cases my Mind leapt over every interval . . . to what I saw was per se a pleasant subject with him (244).

It is clear enough that Keats' part in this interchange is like the intrusion of Pistol, the *feu de joie,* and the rest. At bottom is the loadstone concatenation, the magnet of interlinking. This highly charged mineral Keats probably found (although those who would platonize *Endymion* think he never read Plato) in the *Ion.*[8] Here Socrates explains to the vain rhapsode, who, ignorant of the real nature of poetry, can still render Homer and "bring down the house," that there is a divinity moving him when he performs:

Like that contained in the stone which Euripides calls a magnet, but which is commonly known as the stone of Heraclea. This stone not only attracts iron rings, but also imparts to them a similar power of attracting other rings; and sometimes you may see a number of pieces of iron and rings suspended from one another so as to form quite a long chain; and all of them derive their power of suspension from the original stone.

Keats, as usual, stamps the figure with his own die, assigning to the loadstone the virtue of linking ideas rather than, as in Plato, of linking poet, rhapsode, and audience. But it is in both the source of "poetic madness," which is to say, wild flight of the mind, and as Keats here says in jest, these wild rangings at times inform sober reason and plain talk.

"ABSTRACT IDEAS"

Let us look now at some communications which are neither for fun, nor to such limited purpose, communications which intend to convey complex structures, which are in Keats' fashion, analytical.

> Believe me Haydon your picture is a part of myself— I have ever been too sensible of the labyrinthian path to eminence in Art (judging from Poetry) ever to think I understood the emphasis of Painting. The innumerable compositions and decompositions which take place between the intellect and its thousand materials before it arrives at that trembling delicate and snail-horn perception of Beauty. I know not you[r] many havens of intenseness—nor ever can know them—but for this I hope no[ugh]t you adchieve is lost upon me: for when a Schoolboy the abstract Idea I had of an heroic painting— was what I cannot describe I saw it somewhat sideways large prominent round and colour'd with magnificence —somewhat like the feel I have of Anthony and Cleopatra. Or of Alcibiades, leaning on his Crimson Couch in his Galley, his broad shoulders imperceptibly heaving with the Sea (129).

This extraordinary account of heroic painting is not what we should normally greet as an abstract idea. It is a kind of exfoliation of images, according to principles of relevancy personal to the mind of John Keats. There are two communications, both of which go forward with a kind of mounting speed. Both start from a conventional and communicative arrangement of words, and these proceed in wider and wider arcs of reference until the sense of what one image has to do with the next is all but lost—quite lost, in fact, when we come to Alcibiades' broad shoulders.

To say that Keats here merely moves from literal to progressively metaphorical speech is to oversimplify. To say that these are bad metaphors—disparate items which never fuse—is to beg the question. Messrs. Ogden and Richards, gospel in these matters, inform us that

> metaphor itself need not, as in strict symbolizing be used to bring out or stress a structural feature in a reference, but rather to provide, often under cover of a pretense of this elucidation, new sudden and striking collocations of references, for the sake of the compound effects of contrast, conflict, harmony, interanimation, and equilibrium which may be so attained.

Yet it is doubtful whether these bold collocations should be called metaphors at all, for we have to do here not with recognizable analogy, nor yet with mere effect, either compound or simple; what Keats is doing in this passage, more and more heartily as he goes along, is telling Haydon literally what he thinks about heroic painting. That his thought is imaginal, that it omits colorless relational words, that it is communicative only of itself, is no argument against its relevancy. Psychologists assure us that if we tell what we really think about almost anything, the result will probably be surprising even to ourselves. For the essential processes of thought, it appears, do actually occur in these private regions where images diverse, fragmentary, elusive, and seemingly quite remote from the matter in hand constellate in an infinity of shapes, colors, sounds, attitudes, to receive and organize the energies of the mind. "Not only may we think sensibly," writes Hollingworth,

> in terms of relevant images, conventional words, and standardized gestures. The most miscellaneous details— imagery fragments, perseverating impressions, current sensations—may stand for, represent, symbolize or mean, more portentous primary objects. This we call the vicarious functioning of content. . . . Revived processes of thought of almost any sort, or even present incoming impressions may vicariously function as standard-bearers for any intellectual exploration that may be in progress at the time. Thought may then never be really imageless.
> —*The Psychology of Thought*

Titchener discovered that *but* "means" to him "a bald crown with a fringe of hair below, and a massive black shoulder, the whole passing down the visual field from northwest to southeast." An heroine was "a tall figure, the only clear part of which is a hand holding up a steely grey skirt." Most of us, summary, callous, and habituated as we are in thinking, are not aware of this vicariously functioning content; it is not, in fact, easily accessible. It took Sidgwick a long time to discover that to him *value* "meant" a "faint partial image of a man putting something in a scale." But Keats was not habituated or callous to any kind of experience, and he knew and repeatedly told what he thought and meant in this immediate sense of thinking and meaning. In "Sleep and Poetry" he gives a reason why he must bid farewell to the joys of nymphs and nature. The reason is a chariot and a charioteer, "shapes of delight and mystery," and, to the annoyance of critics, that is all.

Let us turn now to that important letter to Bailey, parts of which we have already quoted, in which he speaks of the simple imaginative mind:

> O I wish I was as certain of the end of all your troubles as that of your momentary start about the authenticity of the Imagination. I am certain of nothing but of the holiness of the Heart's affections and the truth of Imagination— What the imagination seizes as Beauty must be truth—whether it existed before or not—for I have the same Idea of all our Passions as of Love they are all in their sublime, creative of essential Beauty. In a Word, you may know my favorite Speculation by my first Book and the little song I sent in my last—which is a representation from the fancy of the probable mode of operating in these Matters. The Imagination may be compared to Adam's dream—he awoke and found it truth. I am the more zealous in this affair, because I have never yet been able to perceive how any thing can be known for truth by consequitive reasoning—and yet it must be. Can it be that even the greatest Philosopher ever arrived at his goal without putting aside numerous objections. However it may be, O for a Life of Sensations rather than of Thoughts! It is "a Vision in the form of Youth" a Shadow of reality to come—and this consideration has further convinced me for it has come as auxiliary to another favorite Speculation of mine, that we shall enjoy ourselves here after by having what we called happiness on Earth repeated in a finer tone and so repeated. And yet such a fate can only befall those who delight in Sensation rather than hunger as you do after Truth. Adam's dream

will do here and seems to be a conviction that Imagination and its empyreal reflection is the same as human Life and its Spiritual repetition. But as I was saying—the simple imaginative Mind may have its rewards in the repeti[ti]on of its own silent Working coming continually on the Spirit with a fine Suddenness—to compare great things with small—have you never by being Surprised with an old Melody—in a delicious place—by a delicious voice, fe[l]t over again your very Speculations and Surmises at the time it first operated on your Soul—do you not remember forming to yourself the singer's face more beautiful that [*for* than] it was possible and yet with the elevation of the Moment you did not think so—even then you were mounted on the Wings of Imagination so high—that the Prototype must be here after—that delicious face you will see. What a time! I am continually running away from the subject— sure this cannot be exactly the case with a complex Mind —one that is imaginative and at the same time careful of its fruits—who would exist partly on Sensation partly on thought—to whom it is necessary that years should bring the philosophic Mind—such an one I consider your's and therefore it is necessary to your eternal Happiness that you not only ~~have~~ drink this old Wine of Heaven, which I shall call the redigestion of our most ethereal Musings on Earth; but also increase in knowledge and know all things (67–69).

If we can succeed in disentangling the strands of this bright web, we shall learn a great deal both of what and of how Keats thought, for it contains a striking deal both of precept and example. Some of its materials we have already identified. We know that when Keats speaks of the repetitions of the mind's own silent workings coming continually upon

the spirit, he is talking of the incremental effects of the associative process and giving the classic illustration of the songs of
childhood. This is perfectly empirical—scientific—so to
speak. But we see also that Keats fancies this incremental process as continuing beyond the limits of experience into the
"reality to come," that the constantly enhancing beauty of
recollection of things past moves toward a prototype here-
after—"that delicious face you will see." *This,* as we have said,
is not empirical, and seems to be an attempt to optimize and
theologize the imagination in Wordsworthian fashion. Where
Keats got the idea of the prefigurative truth of the imagination, I do not know. It is the kind of notion, obviously, that
would appeal to the divinity student Bailey, and I suspect its
source lies in that fact. The "camelion-poet" is taking a shade
of the color of his correspondent. The context is not really
Wordsworthian, for Keats says that for him it is not necessary
that the years should bring the philosophic mind. This is
Wordsworth's need and phrase, and it is also what Bailey requires. For Keats the simple, imaginative mind will apparently
serve, even in maturity.

And what kind of mind is it? First of all it is *simple,* and is
contrasted with the "complex" mind. This distinction obviously comes from the associationists' discrimination of ideas as
"simple ideas of sensation" and "complex ideas." The simple,
imaginative mind lives a life of sensation. What a deal of ink
has flown over this wish of Keats for a life of sensation, rather
than of thought. It has been cited to convict him of sensuality,
and it has been explained and apologized for and said to have
nothing to do with sensations of the body. The theory of the
association of ideas makes it clear that what Keats means by a

life of sensation, is the life of the imagination, a life solidly
grounded in bygone events of eye, ear, palate, etc., but modi-
fying, refining, and ramifying them into infinitely complex
chains of associates. It is distinguished from thought in that
it operates on these directly, preserving and enhancing their
color and life and form, rather than abstracting and generaliz-
ing them in systems and relations. When Keats calls this life a
vision in the form of youth, he is again speaking as an associationist. The imagination in youth is warm and easily delighted. Wordsworth had spoken of the visionary splendor
with which the objects of sensation were clothed in youth, and,
as we know, Hartley arranged for the imagination's early
death.

The way in which the simple, imaginative mind works on
its sensuous material is clear. It puts aside numerous objections, it is not "consequitive," and not careful of its fruits. It
makes known its speculations by "my first book" and by the
"little song I sent in my last." The first book of *Endymion,* to
which Keats here refers, contains in its dreamy composite
many speculations. We must take Keats' word for it that
among them is the idea that all our passions are creative in
their sublime of essential Beauty. But they are speculations of
the immediate and direct sort that we have seen in the letters.
The "little song sent in my last" is the song of the Indian
Maiden in Book IV:

> O Sorrow,
> Why dost borrow
> The natural hue of health from vermeil lips?—
> To give maiden blushes
> To the white rose bushes?

Or is't thy dewy hand the daisy tips?

．　　．　　．　　．　　．　　．

To Sorrow
I bade good-morrow,
And thought to leave her far away behind;
But cheerly, cheerly,
She loves me dearly;
She is so constant to me, and so kind:
I would deceive her
And so leave her,
But ah! she is so constant and so kind.

"These be very fine lines," said Coleridge of a passage in his "Destiny of Nations," "but hang me if I know, or ever did know the meaning of them." This is a very fine song, especially the second stanza quoted, but it is scarcely an explanation of how the passions create beauty. It is something much more eloquent, "a representative from the fancy of the probable mode of operating in these matters." This is, in fact, precisely what the simple imaginative mind always gives. Its mighty abstract ideas are modes of operation—frankly conveyed—in the "halo or penumbra that surrounds and escorts" the subject. They evolve as the poems evolve from the free work of the associative principle. The striking thing is that Keats dares allow them to stand alone, and without the supporting convention of poetry, that he dares "think" as well as "dream" with his imagination.

"What do you think of heroic painting?"
"I think somewhat sideways, large prominent round, and colored with magnificence."
"What do you think is the highest aim of poetry?"

"I think

"O'ersailing the blue cragginess a car
And steeds with creamy manes."

"How do you know that what the imagination seizes
on as beauty must be truth?"

"Adam's dream will do here."

These are the "sensations" by which the simple, imaginative mind works, and of which it makes its answers. We may, if we find them too direct, flush like the friend, and look angry, or we may find them pleasant subjects per se. They are referable ultimately to sensation, but they are not unphilosophical.

Are they in fact answers at all? Did Keats conceive in them any communicative power or are they merely subjective formulations, another trick of the self-concentrated artist? There is no doubt that Keats believed in the possibility of vital contacts between human beings made in the medium of imagination, a communication between streams of consciousness more intimate and complete than ordinary eclectic utterance. "One of the most mysterious of semi-speculations," he wrote, "is that of one mind imagining into another." This again, is the natural aim of poetry, but Keats was not one to compartmentalize his faculties. We have seen practical instances of imagining into other minds in the disconcerting directness of his answers to the friend who wanted portrait and manuscript. Keats goes about it quite consciously.

"We in this world," he wrote his brother,

merely comp[r]ehend each other in different degrees.
. . . Now the reason why I do not feel at the present moment so far from you is that I remember your Ways and Manners and actions; I known you[r] manner of thinking, your manner of feeling: I know what shape

your joy or your sorrow would take. . . . I shall read a
passage of Shakespeare every Sunday at ten oClock—
you read one at the same time and we shall be as near
each other as blind bodies can be in the same room
(247).

The possible identity of content in minds equipped with the
same association trains was a matter on which both Hartley
and Alison, as we have seen, speculated. Keats was attracted
by the notion that, according to this principle, the actual evolution of a train could be a labor shared. "You know . . .
where I haunt most," he said to Reynolds, "so that if you
think for five minutes after having read this you will find it a
long letter, and see written in the Air above you, Your most
affectionate friend" (115). "Why [on another occasion] be
teased with . . . Wordsworth's 'Matthew with a bough of
wilding in his hand' when we can have Jacques 'under an
oak, &c.'?—The secret of the Bough of Wilding will run
through your head faster than I can write it" (96). And in yet
another letter he invites Reynolds to make "a good wholesome
loaf, with your own leaven . . . of my fragments" (142).

These, then, are two of the virtues of the simple, imaginative mind, in whose intellections Keats allowed powers of the
creative trance to flow: fidelity to the imaginal essence of the
thinking process, and richness and intimacy of communication in the giving out of these images. In attempting to isolate
and analyze them we have had to draw clean distinctions and
simple patterns in matters which common sense reminds were
infinitely fluid, complex, and subtle. But the attempt, if it
has succeeded, has illustrated the fact that imagination, with
fons et origo in sensation, tended to prevail in and pervade
Keats' mind in all its uses.

"To the Eyes of the Man of Imagination Nature is Imagination itself."

—WILLIAM BLAKE

CHAPTER FIVE

BEAUTY
IS TRUTH

W<small>E HAVE CHOSEN</small> to explore Keats' faith in the sensuous, wild, eloquent imagination at seasons of high tide. We have marked it flooding his vision of the ideal bard, or bearing him along in nature trance, or dream, or toward a rich unpacking of the mind in prose. It was evidently an ardent faith, but it was not untroubled. At times he resisted the turbulent energies of the free-ranging mind, took the detached and critical view, and occasionally decided to give over the life of sensation and cultivate instead judgment, knowledge, and philosophy:

> I find cavalier days are gone by. I find that I can have no enjoyment in the World but continual drinking of Knowledge— . . . there is but one way for me—the road lies th[r]ough application study and thought. I will pursue it and to that end purpose retiring for some years. I have been hovering for some time between an exquisite sense of the luxurious and a love for Philosophy —were I calculated for the former I should be glad— but as I am not I shall turn all my soul to the latter (134).

Doubts and misgivings such as these were not infrequent. But it is not our purpose here to weigh them. We are concerned rather with Keats' affirmations; rather to explore the psychological and experiential grounds, and the artistic consequences of his faith when it was strong. And so we have taken Keats at his word when he says he prefers a life of sensation to a life of thought, when he calls his own a "simple imaginative mind," and when he says he cannot see how anything can be known for truth by consecutive reasoning; and we have left the afterthoughts and moments of ebbing conviction for others to perpend. If this seems an arbitrary or partial view of Keats, there is yet this to be said for it, that it keeps us in contact with most of his best, mature work. For the great odes and the great "Eve of St. Agnes" are, in their special way, also products of Keats' faith in the imagination. It is, to be sure, a somewhat tempered imagination which shapes these poems, spontaneous still, and associative, but moving in currents more organic and determined than we have seen. It is an imagination which discovers in its own process a profound principle of structure, conforming, as Keats thought, to the very principle of human experience.

This principle is distilled in a simple, baffling equation, a Tarpeian rock of Keats criticism, which we must now approach.

> Beauty is truth, truth beauty,—that is all
> Ye know on earth, and all ye need to know.

No two lines of Keats' poetry are so famous as these, and I think none so perplexing to his readers. They are generally believed to hold the essence of his creed; yet no one has quite managed to tell what they mean. Though not for lack of effort. There is a sizable literature of learned and critical essays to explain them; to show that he meant, for example, "ecstasy, being beautiful, is truth," or that "the intense moments and significant aspects of life which art holds in silent equipoise" are truth, or that the beauty which Professor Havens saw in the Roman aqueduct at Tarragona is truth. And there have been other attempts to show that the lines are really meaningless, and even unfortunate. This perplexity of opinion is not at all surprising. Keats has stated in these lines an equation, and failed to limit either term. Hence beauty $=$ truth can mean any one of a number of different things. For example:

1. Ugliness is nonexistent.
2. Nature is harmonious.
3. Works of art provide the sole stability in the flux of experience.
4. Courage is the highest virtue.

Moreover, this equation is not original with Keats. In fact it is a commonplace at least as early as Plato, and it falls on the ear already resonant with echoes of traditional meaning and half meaning. It is possible to suspect that Keats had in mind some such vaguely aesthetic or vaguely religious meanings as are suggested in these passages from Shaftesbury and Akenside:

> What is beautiful is harmonious and proportionable; what is harmonious and proportionable is true, and what is at once beautiful and true is of consequence agreeable and good.—"Miscellaneous Reflections"

> Thus then at first was Beauty sent from Heaven
> The lovely ministress of Truth and good
> In this dark world, for truth and good are one
> And beauty dwells in them and they in her.
> —*The Pleasures of Imagination*

There is also the obvious possibility, even likelihood, that whatever meaning the statement carries, it is a meaning impromptu and incomplete, the comment of a philosophical amateur, or at most the product of "such reflection on life and the world as any thoughtful man may practise, a reflection intent, no doubt, but neither technical nor systematic."

Finally, it is certainly possible to suppose that the statement was never intended to convey any meaning at all; that it is merely one of those verbal arrangements made to express and control a state of emotion, subject neither to practical check nor to integration with other valid ideas.

> Stop and consider, life is but a day—

is probably such a statement, or *pseudo statement,* as Mr. I. A. Richards calls them. They are common and valuable in poetry, but it is futile to require that they be "true," or even to ask what they "mean," in the usual sense of meaning. Accordingly, John Middleton Murry begins his speculations on these lines by observing:

> We do not have to ask, coldly, what is the meaning of 'Beauty is Truth.' We have to ask what meaning it could possibly bear to such a man at such a moment in order to assuage his pain.

It is probably wisest not wholly to exclude any of these meanings, or degrees of meaning or types of meaning, in attempting to understand Keats' statement. It seems, in its context, to overflow the channels of logic and demonstration. It is characteristic of Keats' rich and associative mind that his meanings should be multiple, fluent, and blended, rather than discreet and formal, that his best thoughts should be thoughts beyond thought, insights resolving at "the very bourne of conception." He says explicitly, in fact, that the urn leads to this region:

> Thou, silent form, dost tease us out of thought
> As doth eternity.

The possibilities there are infinite, and for this reason perhaps no structure of ideas which we may detect in Keats to make reasonable and definite the equation of truth and beauty will be adequate to reflect the total meaning in his mind, nor explain the full impact of the statement on ours. This obvious fact, however, need not prevent nor make insignificant the effort to locate the reasonable stratum. There is, in fact, a meaning in "Beauty is truth," which is important in Keats' whole development, for it relates (as we have suggested) to those convictions and practices in thought and poetry elsewhere so cogent and so characteristic of him. We propose now to explore it.

"THE SWEET AND BITTER WORLD"

We recall, to begin with, that the statement at the close of the "Urn," although it is the most famous, is not Keats' only assertion of the truth of beauty. "What the imagination seizes as Beauty must be truth," he had written to Bailey in November of 1817. It was a year later that he confessed to his brother George: "I can never feel certain of a truth but from a clear perception of its beauty." The statement with which the "Urn" closes, uttered as it was in the late spring of 1819, is then the third expression of the idea within about a year and a half.

It is also important to realize that the poem of which this statement is climax is not an isolated poem, but stands in specific relationship to other poems. It is, in fact, one of a group of five odes, all written in the space of about a month. All five are homogeneous in mood, with ideas and images that interrelate and recur—a fact sometimes curiously overlooked. Most closely related in time of composition, in poetic substance, and in logical statement are the "Nightingale," "Melancholy," and the "Urn." In this trilogy the middle poem stands as a comment on the experience of beauty in general; the other two give directly and dramatically specific illustrations of this experience. The structure of the events in the "Urn" and in the "Nightingale" conforms precisely to the description in "Melancholy" of all such events.

For the point of "Melancholy" is plainly that the intense experience of joy, beauty, ecstasy carries with it, as inevitably concomitant, an equally intense experience of sadness. Do not, says the poem, seek for essential sadness in events called sad, for these are all heavy and dull with the dross of sorrow.

> For shade to shade will come too drowsily,
>   And drown the wakeful anguish of the soul.

The pungent flavor of sorrow is most richly concentrate at the bottom of the cup of delight:

> She dwells with Beauty—Beauty that must die;
>   And Joy, whose hand is ever at his lips.

And is known to those only who can savor joy and beauty to their last essences. Or, to put it the other way, moments of beauty, of joy, of love, if explored to the full, reveal always the opposite virtue of sorrow.

In that rich moment of beauty which the song of the nightingale supplied him, Keats found accordingly that interblend of joy and anguish which "Melancholy" describes. The ecstasy of the bird's song and the beauty of the odorous night carry drowsy numbness, a cup of dull opiate ("Wolf's-bane, tight-rooted, for its poisonous wine"), even the death-wish. The poem proceeds then in counterpoint. The wings of poesy bear the rapt poet into the forest dim, but they bear also "the weariness, the fever and the fret," the knowledge that men suffer, that youth dies, and love fails. No crasser blunder of criticism has ever been committed, I suppose, than to call the "Nightingale" a poem of romantic escape. From its first enthralling notes, the joyous and immortal chant of the bird carries an undersong of mortality weeping amid alien corn. And at the close the undersong prevails:

> The fancy cannot cheat so well
>   As she is fam'd to do.

This is the real of sadness, as "Melancholy" defines sadness.

In the "Urn" the elements are presented in the same eloquent counterpoise. The joy of the poet in the presence of the urn's silent form is intense indeed, and therefore inevitably fraught with sadness. Mortality weighs heavily as the poet contemplates the bold form of the lover; the "happy boughs" imply less fortunate branches whose leaves fade with the departing year. The love, "forever warm and still to be enjoyed," carries a contrasting sense of human passion, the "heart high sorrowful and cloyed." By the beauty of the nightingale's song and the beauty of the urn, Keats has been led twice into the very temple of Delight, wherein on both occasions he has found Melancholy regally enthroned.

These relationships have been evident to several students of the odes, though, strangely, not to all. It would scarcely seem requisite that Keats add to the list in "Melancholy" of lovely things instinct with sorrow, a nightingale's song and a Greek vase. Had he done so the connection between these three poems would perhaps be unmistakably clear to all.

This is the first thing to note, then, of the "Grecian Urn," that it presents an event of beauty according to a concept of beauty similarly realized in another poem and defined in a third.

This response, artistic practice, comment on life (for it is all three at once) appears again and again in Keats' poetry. The constant kinship of joy to grief brings a cry to the lips of Cynthia in *Endymion*, II,

> Woe! woe! is grief contain'd
> In the very deeps of pleasure.

The song of the Indian Maid in Book IV says somewhat elliptically that it is the fact of sorrow which makes lovely the rose. The reference to "the sweet and bitter world" will be remembered in the gloomy daydream, "Lines Written in the Highlands." Lamia is described as of

sciential brain
To unperplex bliss from its neighbour pain.

Thea in "Hyperion" is

How beautiful, if sorrow had not made
Sorrow more beautiful than Beauty's self.

Significant is the fact that the distinguishing trait of the poet dreamer in "The Fall of Hyperion" is that he cannot experience joy and grief distinct from one another. In such passages is the "truth" of these comminglings attested.

To their beauty, likewise, there is constant witness. In the sonnet "On Seeing the Elgin Marbles for the First Time" we are given a presumably true account of the train of associations arising from an experience of beauty. It is a train moving toward mighty opposites; it

mingles Grecian grandeur with the rude
Wasting of old Time.

The impact of the thing of beauty again includes a sense of inevitable death. And the poem closes on the climactic and eloquent juxtaposition of

A sun—a shadow of a magnitude.

There is very little distinction in such poems as the "Nightingale," the "Grecian Urn," "Melancholy," and the "Elgin Marbles" between the beauty of the poems and Beauty, which is the subject of the poems. Contrasts are inevitable in them, for they at once intend, and are about, beauty; they combine two (or, in "Melancholy," three) kinds of closely parallel illustrations of the nature of beauty. But in other poems, too, where the poet, although consciously creating beauty, is not so explicitly talking about it, we find similar juxtaposition: love and death in the sonnet beginning "Bright star . . . ," verse, fame, beauty, and death in the sonnet, "Why did I laugh . . . ?" "The Eve of St. Agnes" is, as Amy Lowell poetically described it, "a choral hymn . . . not single and melodic but massed and contrapuntal," a study in contrasts of light, dark; cold, warmth; love, hate. One of the most striking juxtapositions occurs at the very end of this poem, where, as the young lovers flee away into the storm to begin their new lives, Angela the old dies palsy-twitched, and the Beadsman

For aye unsought for slept among his ashes cold.

There is something even a little forced, it may be, in this exact and symmetrical coincidence of new love life and death; I have heard it maintained that Keats could never have had in mind a coincidence so crudely improbable, and that the lines do not mean that these aged ones died on the night of the lovers' escape. But the very task of the poet is to create beauty, and beauty at its highest intensity requires these stark oppositions. The law of probability would be waived in accord with this higher law of art and life. In any interpretation, the end of "The Eve of St. Agnes" provides a striking example of Keats' conscious and deliberate bringing together of intense extremes.

The three odes, then, the sonnets referred to, and "The Eve of St. Agnes" are fundamentally alike. All of them are, so to speak, beauty, and in spite of superficial differences, beauty of the same stamp. This beauty, Keats tells us, is truth, and truth this beauty. To seek a literary source for a response to experience so humanly natural, and an artistic practice so accordant with the very purposes of art as the perception and use of contrast, seems in a sense needless and tiresome. The knowledge of the bitter in the sweet of life and of the poignancy of commingled joy and grief is a fact perhaps of universal experience, certainly of common remark through the ages. Lucretius sang of the eternal perishing of things, and of the pain with which love's ecstasies are tinged. St. Augustine told how "sorrowful joys contend with joyful sorrows"; and Shakespeare's sonnets speak the mortality of love and beauty. Thomas Gray observed that

> The hues of Bliss more brightly grow,
> Chastised by abler tints of woe;
> And blended, form with artful strife
> The strength and harmony of Life.

Common also is the awareness of the power of these profound contrasts in art. Burke, in his famous essay, notes how opposed extremes operate to produce the sublime. Coleridge under the influence of Fichte and Schelling made the reconlogical law behind the common experience, did not neglect this fundamental principle of art and mind. Hume regarded contrast as equally fundamental in the associative process with contiguity, resemblance, and causation. Hartley observed that nascent ideas of fear and horror in a peaceful scene enliven all other ideas, and by degrees pass into pleasure by suggesting security from pain. And Alison declared the principle of conciliation of opposites a critical principle.

The associationists, ever trying to formulate the psycho-

trast to be one of the most active in the aesthetic experience.

For Keats' conviction of the significance of contrast, then, we need look to no particular source. But with him the juxtaposition of poignant opposites seems to be integrated with the conviction that beauty is truth, truth beauty, and for this integration, there is, I believe, a rather definite source, namely, the thought and writing of that associationist critic with whom Keats was most familiar, William Hazlitt.

KEATS AND HAZLITT

Keats had, as everyone knows, the profoundest admiration for Hazlitt: ". . . Your only good damner, and if ever I am damn'd—damn me if I shoul'nt like him to damn me." He owned at least two of Hazlitt's books, speaks of reading a third, attended his lectures, walked with him, dined with him, and asked him, or at any rate expressed the intention of asking him, the best metaphysical road to take. Now Hazlitt, writing of Gainsborough, remarks at one point that ". . . he wanted that vigor of intellect which perceives the beauty of truth"; on another occasion, ". . . to the genuine artist truth, nature, beauty are almost different names for the same thing"; elsewhere, "Nature is always truth at its best and beauty and sublimity as well." The words truth and beauty are so constantly coupled in his writing as to be practically a set phrase: "Compared with works like these [Domenichino's "Possessed Boy"], which are the pure mirrors of truth and beauty, Hogarth's subjects are the very measles of art." "The contemplation of truth and beauty is the proper object for which we were created." "Truth with beauty suggests the feeling of immortality." "We seek for truth and beauty wherever we can find them." These are only a few examples. Hazlitt's most considerate statement of the virtual identity of truth and beauty comes at the close of his essay "On the Elgin Marbles." He concludes this essay with ten formal propositions in aesthetics, of which the tenth is: "That truth is to a certain degree beauty and grandeur, since all things are connected, and all things modify one another in nature." The conclusion that truth and beauty are in effect one is supported in Hazlitt by a careful, logical structure, including some rather original conclusions in what Hazlitt called metaphysics. It is obviously likely that Hazlitt's disciple in metaphysical matters—Keats —should have in mind this structure in his own avowals of their identity.

Hazlitt, although in this, as in other matters, heterodox, was definitely associationist in his thoughts about thinking and about beauty. While he broke with the complete materialism of Hartley's theory at points to which we shall at once come, his *Essay on the Principles of Human Action . . . To Which Are Added, Some Remarks on the Systems of Hartley and Helvetius* (which, it will be recalled, Keats owned) mainly accepts and extends the essential concepts of the theory. The vocabulary of association appears constantly also in his criticism of literature and art. Commenting, for example, on Wordsworth's *Excursion,* he writes.

> He exemplifies in an eminent degree the power of *association;* for his poetry has no other source or character. He has dwelt among pastoral scenes till each object has become connected with a thousand feelings, a link in the

chain of thought, a fibre of his own heart.—*The Spirit of the Age,* "Mr. Wordsworth"

In an essay, "On the Prose Style of Poets" he writes that the poet's

> embellishments in his own walk grow out of the subject by natural association; that is, beauty gives way to kindred beauty, grandeur leads the mind on to greater grandeur.

Of his heterodoxies two are interesting to us. One has to do with the manner in which ideas are associated in the mind; the other, with the manner in which objects are perceived. According to Hartley, the process of association was a physical process, depending, as Hazlitt expressed it, "on the mechanical communication of motion from the seat of one idea to that of the next and so on, according to a certain local arrangement of ideas in the brain." To this purely physical concept of mental process, Hazlitt objects. We must, he says, discover laws of the mind in the mind.

> The effect of association depends upon the conjunction of many circumstances, and principles of action, and is not simply determined by the relation of proximity or remoteness between our ideas with respect to time or place. —"Remarks on the Systems of Hartley and Helvetius"

There is, Hazlitt insists, a "thinking principle" which makes connections between ideas—"adapts, combines, reconciles ideas impressed upon it." And it combines them, says Hazlitt, not only according to their contiguity, but also according to the more intellectual principles of similarity and (especially) of contrast. Failure to take sufficiently into account the associative power of contrast was, in Hazlitt's mind, a defect of Hartley's system:

> For [he writes] the very opposition of our feelings, as of heat and cold, frequently produces a transition in the mind from the one to the other. This may be accounted for in a loose way by supposing that the struggle between very opposite feelings, producing a violent and perturbed state of mind, excites attention, and makes the mind more sensible to the shock of the contrary impression to that by which it is preoccupied, as we find that the body is more likely to be affected by opposite extremes, as of heat and cold immediately succeeding and counteracting one another. Be this as it may, all things naturally put us in mind of their contrarieties, cold of heat, day of night, etc.—"Remarks"

The law of contrasts, then, in Hazlitt's opinion, was a fundamental principle of human thought.

It was also, he believed, a fundamental principle in poetry. Hazlitt insists on this, and if I seem to labor the point with overnumerous quotations, I at least shall not belie Hazlitt's own stress. The law of opposites is important to poetry in two ways, only one of which will be considered at the moment. It produces the valued quality of intensity or, as Hazlitt (and Keats) usually preferred to call it, *gusto*:

> Tragic poetry, which is the most impassioned species of it, strives to carry on the feeling to the utmost point of sublimity or pathos, by all the force of comparison or contrast.—"On Poetry in General"

The principle of poetry is a very anti-levelling principle.

It aims at effect, it exists by contrast.—*Characters of Shakespeare's Plays,* "Coriolanus"

One mode in which the dramatic exhibition of passion excites our sympathy without raising our disgust is, that in proportion as it sharpens the edge of calamity and disappointment, it strengthens the desire of good. It enhances our consciousness of the blessing by making us sensible of the magnitude of the loss. The storm of passion lays bare and shows us the rich depths of the human soul: *the whole of our existence, the sum-total of our passions and pursuits,* of that which we desire and that 'which we dread is *brought before us by contrast* [my italics]; the action and reaction are equal; the keenness of immediate suffering gives us only a more intense aspiration after intimate participation with the antagonist world of good, makes us drink deeper the cup of human life.—"On Poetry in General"

This law of contrast was a law of which Mozart, for example, was almost ignorant:

Now we confess that with the single exception of the Ghost scene [in Don Giovanni] we not only do not feel any such general character of grand or strongly-contrasted expression pervading the composition, but we do not see any opportunity for it.—*A View of the English Stage*

Spenser, on the other hand, and Shakespeare understood its force; indeed their romantic quality was largely derived from it:

Florimel in Spenser, where she is described as sitting on the ground in the Witch's hut is not classical, though in the highest degree poetical and romantic: for the inci-

dents and situation are in themselves mean and disagree-
able, till they are redeemed by the genius of the poet, and
converted by the very contrast into a source of the utmost
pathos and elevation of sentiment.—"Schlegel on the
Drama"

Hazlitt praises *Macbeth* as written "on a stronger and more
systematic principle of contrast" than any of Shakespeare's
other plays. Of the lines beginning, "How far that little
candle," he writes:

> The image here is one of artificial life; but it is connected
> with natural circumstances and romantic interests, with
> darkness, with silence, with distance, with privation and
> uncertain danger. . . . It is not the splendour of the
> candle itself, but the contrast to the gloom without,—
> the comfort, the relief it holds out from afar to the be-
> nighted traveller—the conflict between nature and the
> first and cheapest resources of art, that constitutes the ro-
> mantic and imaginary, that is, the poetical interest in
> that familiar but striking image.—"Pope, Lord Byron,
> and Mr. Bowles"

One more quotation before turning to other matters. Compar-
ing the arts of Sophocles and Shakespeare, Hazlitt writes:

> The principle of the one is simplicity and harmony, of
> the other richness and power. . . . The one owes its
> charm to a certain union and regularity of feeling, the
> other adds to its effects from complexity, and the com-
> bination of the greatest extremes. The classical appeals to
> sense and habit; the Gothic or romantic strikes from
> novelty, strangeness and contrast. . . . And to exclude
> either one or the other from poetry or art is to deny the

existence of the first principles of the human mind.—
"On the Spirit of Ancient and Modern Literature"

Intensity, then, the romantic intensity of Keats' models, Spenser and Shakespeare, is largely attained through the effect of contrast. Contrast, as I have noted above, serves another important purpose in art. But in order to understand it, we must first take notice of Hazlitt's other heresy to the psychology of his time, which is his theory of perception.

We have seen that the mind, according to Hartley, was composed of simple sensations, ideas of sensation, and complex ideas. The associative power combined ideas of sensation into complex ideas. But pure sensations, that is, perceptions of isolated units of sense experience, were the basis of the whole system. Now Hazlitt believed there were no such things as pure sensations of isolated objects:

> every particular object (even of sense) is an aggregate composed of many parts, and those parts strictly again of others, and so on without end, and therefore all the mind can do in any case is to form a general or abstract idea of the effect of all these together, since to have a perfect idea of each, it must descend into infinite detail, which is impossible.—"Outlines of the Human Mind"

Condillac and Tooke had proved that abstractions are merely verbal. Hazlitt countered by maintaining that all experiences, even those of the simplest objects of sense, involve abstraction:

> All our notions from first to last are, strictly speaking, general and abstract, not absolute and particular; and to have a perfectly distinct idea of any one individual thing, or concrete existence, either as to the parts of which it is composed, or the differences belonging to it, or the cir-

cumstances connected with it would imply an unlimited power of comprehension in the human mind, which is impossible. All particular things consist of and lead to an infinite number of other things. Abstraction is a consequence of the limitation of the comprehensive faculty, and mixes itself more or less with every act of the mind of whatever kind.—"On Abstract Ideas"

All objects of sense perception, even the simplest objects, are, according to Hazlitt, in fact, microcosms. Naturally, in the perception of most units of ordinary experience, we do not follow very far along the path whereby "all things consist of and lead to an infinite number of other things." There is not time enough in life for this. Rather we summarize by means of abstraction and generalization; we perceive a carpet, to use Hazlitt's example, but we do not stop to perceive each thread.

But in the experience of an object of natural beauty, or a work of art, and in the creation of the latter, the situation is different. It is the very perception of the rich web of associated ideas that our apprehension of beauty consists; it is in the chain of relationships suggested by the artist that his power lies. Again Hazlitt's reiteration must justify the number of quotations:

> I have in a former essay ascertained one principle of taste or excellence in the arts of imitation, where it was shown that objects of sense are not, as it were, simple and self evident propositions, but admit of endless analysis and the most subtle investigation. We do not see nature with out eyes, but with our understandings and our hearts. To suppose that we see the whole of any object merely by looking at it is a vulgar error; we fancy we do

because we are, of course, conscious of no more than we
see in it, but this circle of our knowledge enlarges with
further acquaintance and study, and then we perceive
that what we perhaps barely distinguished in the gross
or regarded as a dull blank is full of beauty, meaning and
curious details. He sees most of nature who understands
its language best, or connects one thing with the greatest
number of other things.—"Outlines of Taste"

Imagination consists in enriching one idea by another
which has the same feeling or set of associations belonging to it in a higher or more striking degree.—*Lectures
on the Age of Elizabeth*, "On Miscellaneous Poems, etc."

To see or imitate any given sensible object is one thing,
the effect of attention and practice; but to give expression
to a face is to collect its meaning from a thousand other
sources, is to bring into play the association and feeling
of one's whole life, or an infinity of knowledge bearing
upon a single object.—"On a Portrait of an English
Lady by Vandyke"

The real meaning of Hazlitt's tenth proposition, "that
truth is to a certain degree beauty and grandeur, since all
things are connected, and all things modify one another in
nature," is now clearer. Truth is beauty, beauty truth in the
literal quantitative sense, since beauty is that which brings
into play "the associations and feelings of a whole life," "an
infinity of knowledge bearing upon a single object." There is
evidently no great distinction between "nature" in the sense in
which Hazlitt used it in the paragraph just quoted, and
"truth"; and the understanding of nature, says Hazlitt, is
reserved to him "who connects one thing with the greatest

number of other things"—the creator and perceiver of beauty.

At all events, a work of art was to William Hazlitt a universe, and the experience of this universe by a true appreciator of art, a process extensive in time and cumulative in force. Hazlitt was fond of expressing this idea by the figure of a circle of associated ideas which finally encloses the entire universe. This figure probably derives from the oft-mentioned "great circuit" of fancy, a traditional metaphor whereby Cotton, Akenside, Cowper, and others sought to emphasize the scope and range of the poet's mind, but in Hazlitt it is a specifically associative process, and it is productive of knowledge. "This circle of our knowledge enlarges with further acquaintance. . . ." In praise of Homer and Shakespeare, he writes: "The power of imagination in them is the representative power of all nature. It has its center in the human soul, and makes the circuit of the universe." Elsewhere: "Art is the microscope of the mind, which sharpens the wit as the other does the sight; and converts every object into a little universe in itself. . . . To the genuine artist, truth, nature, beauty, are almost different names for the same thing" ("On Imitation").

To this theory of truth-in-beauty there are two objections: one, that it is purely quantitative, with no description of the nature of the universe evolving from a work of art; the other, that to follow these associations to a point where we approach infinite knowledge—truth—is practically impossible, requiring, in Hazlitt's phrase, "an unlimited power of comprehension in the mind." Hazlitt is aware of both objections. To the former he has evidently no satisfactory answer. At times his remarks would indicate a belief that the universe which a thing of beauty reflects conforms to an ideally true plan, or at least to an objectively true one. "Poetry," he says, "is a fanciful structure, but a fanciful structure raised on the ground-work of the strongest and most intimate associations of our ideas; otherwise it is good for nothing. . . ." And again: ". . . It is in the subordination of the uncertain and superficial combinations of fancy to the more stable and powerful laws of reality that the perfection of art exists." In his notice of Byron's *Letter . . . on the Rev. W. L. Bowles' Strictures . . . ,* Hazlitt writes:

> A pack of cards, a silver bodkin, a paste buckle may be imbued with as much mock poetry as you please by lending false associations to it, but real poetry, or the poetry of the highest order, can only be produced by unravelling the real web of associations which have been wound around any subject by nature, and the unavoidable conditions of humanity.

But such affirmations are rare, and they seem belied by remarks such as: "We confess, on the subject of beauty, we are half disposed to fall into the mysticism of Raphael Mengs, who has some notion about a principle of *universal harmony,* if we did not dread the censure of an eminent critic"; or, "I never could make much of the subject of real relations in nature."

For meeting the second obligation Hazlitt is, however, better provided. There is a resource available to the artist which, providing as it does a series of opposite poles on the circumference of the artistic universe, carries by inference the sense of the infinite particulars of which the whole round consists, and this is the principle of contrast. By the use of this fundamental law of the mind, the cosmic circle evolving from a thing of beauty may be swiftly implied. In a passage quoted more fully awhile back occurred these words: "the whole of our existence, the sum-total of our passions and pursuits, of that which we desire and that which we dread is brought before us by contrast." Hazlitt finds Shakespeare using contrast for precisely this purpose. "Shakespeare's imagination," he writes, "is rapid and devious. It unites the most opposite extremes, or as Puck says, in boasting of his own feats, puts a girdle about the earth in forty minutes." Describing Kean's acting of Othello: "It is bestriding the microcosm of man like a Colossus, and by uniting the extremes of being, seemingly implies all the intermediate links." The idea appears again without the figure, in the statement, "To explain the nature of laughter and tears is to account for the condition of human life, for it is in a manner compounded of these two" ("On Wit and Humour").

Beauty, then, in the infinity of the associations it evokes, is truth. Polar opposites suggest this infinity by a kind of artistic shorthand. They serve, although Hazlitt does not expressly say so, approximately the same function in the perception of beauty that abstraction serves in ordinary perception. They are poignantly present in actual life; they are the manifestation of a great law of the mind; they produce the greatest intensity in art.

We are "borne darkly, fearfully afar" from Keats and in order to get back to him we must recross the considerable space between the journalist-critic—all theory, precept, and abstraction—and the poet whose reasonings substantiate in solid poems. In Hazlitt the special theory of perception, the infinite associations inherent in beauty, the suggestive and intense power of contrast, and the identity of truth and beauty are related by discernible logical links. In Keats these ideas appear compacted in poems, or they occur separately, as in his comment on *Paradise Lost,* that "there is a greatness which [it] possesses over every other poem—the *Magnitude of Contrast* [Keats' italics]." Or, if they are juxtaposed, the relationship between them is not defined, as in the following:

> The excellence of every art is its intensity, capable of making all disagreeables evaporate, from their being in close relationship with Beauty and Truth. Examine "King Lear," and you will find this exemplified through-out; but in this picture [West's "Death on the Pale Horse"] we have unpleasantness without any momentous depth of speculation excited, in which to bury its repulsiveness (71).

This comment is reminiscent of Hazlitt's remarks, quoted above, explaining how "the dramatic exhibition of passion excites our sympathy without causing our disgust. . . . The whole of our existence is brought before us by contrast." The derivation of the ideas from Hazlitt and the fact of their interrelation in Keats' mind is suggested in this passage from a letter to Bailey:

> It is an old maxim of mine and of course must be well known that every point of thought is the centre of an intellectual world—the two uppermost thoughts in a Man's mind are the two poles of his World he revolves on them and every thing is southward or northward to

him through their means. We take but three steps from feathers to iron (112).

Here in Keats' phrases and with his own characteristic twist is Hazlitt's theory of perception—any idea (or sensation, or idea of sensation) a microcosm. And here also, although in curiously illogical sequence, is the theory (logical in Hazlitt) of contrast—feathers to iron.

To appreciate the work of art, says Hazlitt, we must brood upon it, allowing thought to suggest thought, beauty to suggest beauty, until the profound meaning, the infinite associations unfold in a round universe of knowledge and delight. In the creation of art, the master unites opposite extremes of this universe, and so suggests the intervening segments of the arc. Brooding upon things of beauty we have seen to be the very dynamic of Keats' imagination. We have already quoted the letter to Reynolds telling how any one grand and spiritual passage serves him as a starting point toward all "the two and thirty palaces." And Hazlitt's figure of the circle emerges as the letter proceeds:

> A strain of music conducts to an odd angle of the Isle and when the leaves whisper, it puts a girdle round the earth.

But Keats must ever restamp and recreate, and the circle becomes a polygon, a spider web.

> Memory should not be called knowledge. . . . It appears to me that almost any Man may like the spider spin from his own inwards his own airy Citadel—the points of leaves and twigs on which the spider begins her work are few, and she fills the air with a beautiful circuiting.

Man should be content with as few points to tip with the fine Web of his Soul, and weave a tapestry empyrean full of symbols for his spiritual eye, of softness for his spiritual touch, of space for his wandering, of distinctness for his luxury. But the Minds of Mortals are so different and bent on such diverse journeys that it may at first appear impossible for any common taste and fellowship to exist between two or three under these suppositions. It is however quite the contrary. Minds would leave each other in contrary directions, traverse each other in numberless points, and at last greet each other at the journey's end. An old Man and a child would talk together and the old Man be led on his path and the child left thinking (103).

There is little doubt, I think, that the path along which this beautifully realized pair converse is the path whereby "all things lead to an infinite number of other things," "an infinitude of knowledge bearing upon a single point." It is the great circle of imagination, on whose vast arc the associating mind continues its indolent voyage, in waking or sleep, prompted by natural or wrought beauty, wafted on by chance breathing of wise or wistful talk, airs of music, or the fanning of boughs. Among the meanings of "Beauty is truth, truth beauty" this meaning, affirmed and rationalized by Hazlitt's association aesthetics, is active.

PROOF ON THE PULSES

Let us now return to poetry. The "Ode on a Grecian Urn" is a much complained-of poem. It is said to be abrupt and incoherent—that its parts do not fit together. The first stanza, we are told, treats of the arrest of beauty in the figures of the urn. Evidently it is a physical beauty which is captured, of men pursuing maidens in ecstasy. But the second stanza opens with an implied repudiation of physical in favor of spiritual beauty:

> Heard melodies are sweet, but those unheard
> Are sweeter.

The rest of this and the whole of the next stanza then treat of the deathlessness of the urn's beauty in contrast with the mortality of beauty in the actual world. The fourth stanza returns to describe another lovely scene on the vase, finding sadness in the fancied desolation of the little town. The final stanza is said to present the urn as a stimulus to profound thought, concluding with the unanticipated and startling announcement that truth is beauty. To this conclusion, as we have seen, Keats was led in his thinking by Hazlitt along logical routes of thought. But in the poem, also, the statement is arrived at logically. It is, of course, the logic of the aesthetic experience, elastic perhaps and easily mistaken for caprice, but unswerving in its own manner of movement.

As we begin to examine it, one curious fact immediately strikes the attention, namely, that though the urn is an object of plastic art, and the beauty of this object is the point of the poem, there is scarcely a word about the formal, physical beauty of the vase in the whole poem. It is called "a fair attitude," and an "Attic shape," but of the beauty of its lines, proportions, colors, we hear no more. And as we proceed we discover that to Keats, as indeed to the art critics of his generation, beauty of pictures and sculpture meant chiefly the power of the object to stimulate the imagination, to start the train of associated ideas. However mistaken this notion, it is clear that for Keats the beauty of the urn resided in the impulse which it gave his mind toward "the two and thirty palaces." This is, in fact, the point of the poem, and it is developed in a perfectly unbroken progression.

The opening two lines say only one thing, that the urn is mute:

> Thou still unravish'd bride of quietness,
>   Thou foster-child of silence and slow time.

It is a perfectly inanimate physical object, presenting its stimuli ostensibly to the eye alone. There follows then the comment upon its eloquence, greater, as the poet feels at the moment, than poetry itself—how it tells its flowery tale "more sweetly than our rhyme." At this point we begin to hear of the actual appearances on the urn, but never directly nor for their own sake. The mind of the poet observes the leafy band around the top only to read in its foliage legends "of deities or mortals, or of both." His remark of the urn's figures takes immediately the form of speculations on their identity, on what they are doing and why. And with consciousness of the "abstractions" to which this sensible object has already carried him, Keats begins the second stanza with the statement that the impact of this mute, physical object is by no means merely physical. Rather its pictured pipes emit a music less sensuous than music's self. From the solid, visible stimulus are vibrating the spirit ditties of no tone. Then for the next two and one-half stanzas we hear their harmonies of sweet and bitter; love and death, the pathos of fulfilled and of never realized love, the joyful vitality of the festal scene, the empty village left silent forever. But the tragic sense of life's paradox has led the mind too far. It returns on an impulse toward reassurance, to the material urn. The men and maidens again become marble, the forest branch and trodden weed images graven in stone. And with this return comes the wondering realization of the distance to which his voyage of conception has borne him— as far as to the uttermost verge of the mind. A familiar region, however: "Many a man can travel to the very bourne of heaven, and yet want confidence to put down his half-seeing." Pan in *Endymion* was the lodge

> For solitary thinkings; such as dodge
> Conception to the very bourne of heaven.

And he rhymed to Reynolds of things that "tease us out of thought." The concussion of the urn's polar symbols, points of pain and delight on the great circle of experiences, leaves him wordless. Of this mighty paradox which the urn proposes, there is nothing to be said save that it is. And with a boldness partaking of despair he dares the proposition in aesthetics, the generalization *de natura rerum:* That the world is terrible and beautiful, that attainment and loss are one, that time slays as it endows love and laughter. The ever-lovely urn, itself a kind of perpetual counterpoise to the world's woe, will still affirm this truth, the sole truth vouchsafed to man; and, since it perpetually returns the mind to beauty, a truth sufficient to him.

Tradition of common sense and common remark, and the aesthetic reasonings derived from William Hazlitt, go into the composition of meanings in "Beauty is truth, truth beauty," into the meaning of the poem as a whole, and into the other poems illustrative of the truth and beauty of contrasts.

But the cogent testimony was of the pulses, beating the moments of his brief life. "Gorge the honey of life," he wrote to Reynolds from the room where Tom lay. "I pity you as much that it cannot last forever, as I do myself now drinking bitters." Tom was dead in little more than a month, but tempering, mingling in Keats' grief, was new love, this love itself half pain. "This is the world," he writes to his brother the following spring, "Circumstances are like Clouds continually gathering and bursting— While we are laughing the seed of some trouble is put into the wide arable land of events—while we are laughing it sprouts is [*for* it] grows and suddenly bears a poison fruit which we must pluck." And a month later he speaks of the rose to which death is native as its beauty. Love and death attained in the same hour is a consummation longed for in his letters to his sweetheart. Life's terrible and beautiful "truth" crowded his latter years. But it is in the painful last letter to Brown that the axiom comes ultimately home, the theme of contrasts like a leitmotiv, recalled for one final statement, emerging yet with brave, faint overtones of laughter even in the desperate coda of "posthumous existence."

> There is one thought enough to kill me; I have been
> well, healthy, alert, &c., walking with her, and now—
> the knowledge of contrast, feeling for light and shade,
> all that information (primitive sense) necessary for a
> poem, are great enemies to the recovery of the stomach
> (527).

Stark opposites, bitterly true in John Keats' life, and primitive truth and beauty in his poetry.

"Man should not dispute or assert but whisper results to his neighbor. . . ."

—JOHN KEATS

CHAPTER SIX

CONCLUSIONS

 Ⓣ ʜɪs is a golden rule for critics, and invaluable for critics of Keats. The creative process is a complex mystery. Although Keats provides some rather emphatic hints as to his own way of working, they lead us not to "fixities and definites," but rather toward an emphasis and a tendency. In an exploration of his elusive and expressive mind dogma is vain and complete objectivity hardly to be attained. He spoke freely and of many things, but behind the sheen of his language is a reticence whereby the precise relationships and delicate shadings of his thought are often withheld. His odd sleight of words plays along the verges of the inexpressible. Our conclusions, then, will properly be regarded as offering reasonable interpretation rather than as asserting palpable fact. It remains briefly to review them.

We have explained the restless and wild energies of the early poems, the luxuriant tracery of *Endymion* and the sensuous thought of the letters as records in part of Keats' adventures in the subliminal regions of his mind. We have seen that with him the convention of the nature-inspired bard uttering visionary "truth" under the spell of a power higher than reason became a fact of creative experience. It was proved on his pulses as a mode of composition involving surrender in a marked, although of course not precisely measurable, degree to the spontaneous impulse of the mind, and the presentation, at least pseudo-literal, of the thus emergent ideas as poetry. We have seen that this manner of composition was recognized and at times reprehended by his contemporaries. Keats' interest and faith in the spontaneous and extrarational action of the mind was in all probability not naïve nor entirely independent, for the thought and idiom of his day was full of reference to the association of ideas. His early poems of response to natural beauty conform to the pattern for such responses implied by Hartley, and described by the associationist Alison.

The operation of the mind in dreams was a subject of special interest in the psychological thought of his time, and so it was with Keats. He was a devotee of sleep, and his *Endymion* takes much of the form and substance of its intermittent allegory from the action of the dreaming mind. Contemporary psychology assured him that swarmings to the mind of ideas originally derived from sensations comprised the very faculty of the imagination. And in the imagination so conceived Keats had persistent if not constant faith; such faith, indeed, that he extended the use of this faculty to prose communications of "abstract" ideas. From this use his letters take much of their cryptic opulence.

Finally, in a light partly derived from Hazlitt, Keats saw the paradoxical possibility of form in the wild, spontaneous ranging of thought—how, without constraint, the animate, sensuous imagination could be led to equilibrium in the contemplation of profound opposites, its intense aspiring spirit preserved, its letter made legible. And on this point of discovery, as I believe, converged and resolved those tormenting conflicts

194

between imagination and judgment, luxury and philosophy, sensation and thought, to which other writers on Keats have given so much care. At this point death resolved all opposites in its own cold counterpoise.

In arriving at these conclusions we have concentrated on a few poems and ignored certain others. "Lamia" and the two "Hyperion" poems, for example, we have given but passing notice, and "Isabella" none at all. Nor have we undertaken any study of manuscripts, those records of revised and forsaken thoughts, usually considered the surest key to a poet's method of composing. These and other omissions prevent any claims for this study as a complete survey of Keats' mind; they do not, I believe, invalidate it, nor indicate an intention to distort truth by ignoring recalcitrant evidence. The use of mind and view of the imagination herein held characteristic are characteristics of degree, not of kind. It is natural that they should be visible in some poems, and not in all. The inconsequent early poems, the dreamy *Endymion,* and the contrapuntal odes best reveal them, and were hence most studied. But even "Lamia" and the two poems about Hyperion, although they are neither poems of obviously free-ranging thought, nor of contrapuntal design, refer in their allegories to the luxuries and the sufferings of the sensuous imagination. To assume of any poem of Keats, even the most carefully ordered, that the sensuous and wild imagination had no part in its making is obviously rash. There are, as we have noticed, countless stages of composition, and no doubt the demoniac energies at times disguise themselves in sober garb. Many of Keats' manuscripts have already been closely studied by M. R. Ridley in *Keats' Craftsmanship.* The evidence which he has carefully presented of Keats' mode of writing down and revising is not in any way contradicted by the views presented here.

As to the value of this study toward a better understanding of Keats a remark or two will serve. It should conduce, I think, to a more sympathetic reading of the earlier poems. "I stood tip-toe upon a little hill" and "Sleep and Poetry" we may call youthful experiments, and perhaps unsuccessful ones, but it is obviously quite pointless to dismiss their wild beauties as "indolent pasturing on the vegetation of life," or to complain of Keats' "effeminacy" of mind. The dreamy fantasy of *Endymion* may perhaps also be more fully enjoyed when this is accepted as the intended and essential quality of the poem. The search for allegory is not inhibited by the interpretation of *Endymion* as a poem moving in the ways of dream, but there is suggested a less labored and schematic kind of allegorizing. The letters emerge in even greater brilliance when we realize that in them Keats often practices what has been described in the writing of T. S. Eliot as "felt thought," and that they may in many passages be best read as we read modernist poetry. A further emphasis upon the interrelations of the great odes, and another stratum of meaning for the "Grecian Urn" have perhaps evident uses.

Finally, a word on the value to Keats of the practice and views we have ascribed to him: The usual course of an artist's development is from spontaneous overflowing toward discipline and restraint. The wild creative impulse of youth is gradually tempered and fortified by ripening critical power and mature self-control. And the critic observing this course greets the increase of the austerer faculties as the final validation of genius. They emerge as a kind of happy denouement in the usual story of a poet's mind. For this emphasis there is no doubt ample justification. Yet I believe it sometimes carries a tendency to undervalue the youthful effusions, to deplore their excesses, and apologize for them as *jugendsünde*. It is in excess that poetry takes its springs and in tumult (whether or not the gods approve) that the depths are discovered. The critical and inhibiting powers, although essential to the poet, do not identify him. Exuberance is his mark.

I am sure, at any rate, that Keats' experiments in unchanneled thought were of greatest value to him. To whatever specific failures in poetry his aesthetic led him, it loosened and freed his mind. He learned that the native vigor of his sense was an endowment of mind as well as of body, learned of the continuity and community of faculties. He learned to get at the levels of experience whence poetry, with or without the consent of the poet, takes its rise. He learned a bold way with words, and that communications become profound at the point at which they fail. This was good knowledge for a poet.

And by these paths he arrived at the final comment that Beauty is Truth. It was a simple comment on which Keats rested, a brief and sweeping description of the nature of things, not proof against cavil. But in times of evil and pain, when youth and death walk close together, a belief that anguish exists in counterpoise—indeed, by virtue of joy and love—is of ponderable value.

NOTES

Page 14

1. Fuller's remarks on the fancy are quoted by Sidney Colvin in *John Keats: His Life and Poetry: His Friends, Critics, and After-Fame*, p. 389. Colvin suspects that this passage from *The Holy State*, printed in Hunt's *Reflector*, and reprinted by Lamb in his *Specimens*, may have provided Keats the impulse for his poem, "Fancy."

Page 28

2. Quoted by Finney, p. 187.

Page 30

3. Ellis' account of Wilkinson in *The Philosophy of Conflict and Other Essays in War-Time* is noted by Freud, *Gesammelte Schriften*, VI, 139–140.

Page 31

4. A very valuable account of the genesis of this poem is given by B. Ifor Evans, "Keats's Approach to the Chapman Sonnet," *Essays and Studies by Members of the English Association*, XVI (1931), 26–52.

Page 54

5. In his Preface Hartley says that "about eighteen years ago," as the result of reading Gay's "Dissertation Concerning the Principle and Criterion of Virtue" (prefixed to Law's translation of King's *Origin of Evil*), he began to consider the power of association. Some time prior to the *Observations* he had published *Conjecturae quaedam de sensu motu et idearum generatione*, setting forth concisely an association psychology.

Page 67

6. Alison in this passage is quoting from Whately's *Observations on Gardening*.

199

Page 143

7. Stephen Pepper, *Aesthetic Quality* (1937), p. 39. In *Art as Experience* John Dewey writes as follows: "The material of the fine arts consists of qualities; that of experience having intellectual conclusion are signs or symbols having no intrinsic quality of their own, but standing for things that may in another experience be qualitatively experienced. The difference is enormous." One may conclude that what Dewey means by this language is approximate to the somewhat clearer statement of Max Eastman, in *The Enjoyment of Poetry,* "Children are poetic. They love to feel things."

Page 149

8. I am indebted to Professor Donald Mackay for calling to my attention the Platonic ring of Keats' phrase.

INDEX